GOLDEN HART GUIDES
CORNWALL

GOLDEN HART GUIDES

Cornwall

Andrew Franklin & Paul Watkins

SIDGWICK & JACKSON LONDON
in association with Trusthouse Forte

The publishers gratefully acknowledge
the co-operation of Mr H.L.Douch
and the Cornwall Tourist Board
for their assistance and advice

Front cover photo: Fowey
Back cover photo: Bedruthan Steps
Frontispiece: Land's End

Photographs by the British Tourist
Authority, with the exception of
ps 11, 14 (Mansell Collection) 34, 47, 54-55,
58-59, 63 (Lawrence Lawry) 94 (John Piper)

Compiled and designed by Paul Watkins
Editorial assistant: Andrew Franklin

First published in Great Britain 1983
by Sidgwick & Jackson in association
with Trusthouse Forte

ISBN 0-283-98912-2

Photoset by Robcroft Ltd, London WC1
Printed and bound in Great Britain
by Hazell Watson and Viney Limited,
Aylesbury, Bucks
for Sidgwick & Jackson Limited,
1 Tavistock Chambers, Bloomsbury Way,
London WC1A 2SG

Contents

Introduction

St Michael's Mount

Jutting out into the Atlantic Ocean, England's southernmost and westernmost county has a magnificent coastline of 270 miles. Traditionally more accessible by sea than by land, modern communications have done little to change Cornwall's sense of remoteness. Most visitors still have long journeys through more crowded parts of England to get here, and for many the 'difference' of Cornwall – essentially that remoteness – is its greatest attraction. There are, however, many other features which give this county its special appeal.

With its shores nursed by the Gulf Stream, Cornwall is blessed by a gentle climate. Summers are warm and sunny, and the sun sets 20 minutes later in Penzance than in London. In winter heavy frosts and snows are unusual, though not unknown. Cornwall's flowers bloom early, and exotic plants which are rare elsewhere grow in abundance. There are daffodils in February and hedges of fuchsia in early summer; palm trees flourish in Penzance's Morrab Gardens.

Most people visit Cornwall for the scenery, and the Duchy certainly has more than its share of beautiful places. Its greatest asset is the coastline, much of it now protected by the National Trust. The north coast – historically a graveyard for shipping – has superb sandy beaches between the cliffs. The south coast is gentler with wooded estuaries and creeks. It all offers endless pleasures to walkers, swimmers, surfers, yachtsmen and fishermen.

Visitors sometimes forget how much there is to see away from the coast, from the empty and mysterious Bodmin Moor to the Penwith peninsula (the area west of Penzance), covered in more prehistoric monuments than any other part of the country. Wild Bodmin and the area around it is King Arthur country, with its remote and dramatic sites haunted by the legend. Cornwall's villages and towns, too, have a unique character. Often centred around a medieval church named after a local saint, they consist of thatched or slate-hung cob cottages, which over the centuries have merged harmoniously with the landscape. Many are so old they are impossible to date. Even the old mining buildings enhance rather than mar the scene. Romantic decaying ruins, they are reminders of past wealth and industry.

Although it is the scenery and beaches which – deservedly – attract most people, there is much more besides. There are villages and beauty spots to be visited, on foot or by car, great country houses and museums of the Cornish heritage, leisure parks and model railways. For those interested in regional specialities there is the potent local mead, the thick Cornish ice cream and the ubiquitous pasties.

Details of all these attractions and activities are in 'The Best of the Region' section of this book, together with a selection of walks and motoring tours. The Gazetteer lists the principal places of interest in the county, and it is hoped that this guide will make a visit to Britain's 'Far West' all the more enjoyable.

Cornwall

A Brief History

19th-century Sennen

In addition to its remoteness from the rest of the country, Cornwall has a natural barrier, the River Tamar, which rises within five miles of the north coast and flows into the English Channel on the south. It is not surprising, therefore, that Cornwall's earliest settlers came by sea rather than land. The arrival of the Celts (5th century BC) established the character of Cornwall's population on which the subsequent Roman and Anglo-Saxon occupations of Britain had little impact.

Prehistory Cornwall has been inhabited for at least 7000 years and has more monuments – prehistoric forts, menhirs, stone circles, barrows and quoits – than any other county to prove it. Most familiar relics of the Neolithic era are the henges (such as the Stripple Stones on Bodmin Moor) and the vast chamber tombs or quoits. These mass-graves (up to 50 bodies were sometimes buried simultaneously) were made of four or five vast granite blocks erected vertically with a capstone (roof) on top. Originally the whole quoit would have been covered with a mound of earth, but all are now exposed as a result of wind and rain or the work of grave robbers.

With the Bronze Age came the first use of metal and so the rudimentary beginnings of Britain's oldest industry – tin mining. The ore was not extracted underground but 'streamed' or washed from river beds in a process similar to panning for gold. Tin was exported to the Mediterranean, possibly even by the Phoenicians in their high-prowed long-boats. The priceless Rillaton Cup, found during excavations on Bodmin Moor in the 19th c., worked in gold and possibly of Mycenaean origin, is evidence of the trade. (The cup is one of the treasures of the British Museum in London but there is a replica in the County Museum in Truro.) A more extensive legacy from the period are the hundreds of burial barrows scattered all over the county.

From c. 500 BC the first Celts swept into the peninsula from the continent. With their iron tools and weapons they quickly overran the area and established an ascendancy which remained unchallenged – even by the Romans. The warlike tribes built the strategically placed forts which still surmount Cornwall's hills and headlands (examples are at Castle Dore near Fowey, Castle-an-Dinas near St Columb Major and Gurnard's Head near Zennor). However, they also maintained the tin trade, and settlements for these miners-cum-farmers have been discovered. Over 40 have been identified, and two on Penwith (Carn Euny and Chysauster) excavated.

The Romans had little impact on Cornwall. Their last outpost of civilisation – a theatre and hot baths – was at Isca (Exeter). In Cornwall only one Roman villa has been found, and that a simple one devoid of the luxuries of the grand merchants' houses excavated in the south-east. There were three Roman roads into Cornwall (inscribed milestones have been found at Tintagel, Boscastle and near Redruth) but their purpose was not apparently to extend Roman rule but for transporting the tin traded with the Celts who continued to be governed by their kings and tribal chiefs. However, before their departure in 410 AD the Romans had brought one significant change to the population, replacing the Celts' Druidic cults with the new faith that had been adopted by the world's greatest empire: Christianity.

Early Christianity Within a century of the Romans' departure, a number of Welsh, Breton and particularly Irish missionaries had made their way to Cornwall. This was the 'Coming of the Saints'. Some sailed to Cornwall, others like St Piran arrived by millstone. St Ia came on a leaf. Once in Cornwall, in addition to performing the miracles necessary for canonisation, the saint-missionaries established oratories and small monasteries. Often these were on much older sites of Druidical importance. The buildings were crude, generally only constructed from mud and rubble.(A remarkable surviving example of an Early Christian oratory is that of St Piran near Perranporth, buried under the sand dunes for many centuries.)

The oratories may have had small altars, but often a holy well or an inscribed stone, with runic or dog-latin inscriptions, served as the focus for religious activity. From the 8th century the stones were superseded by Celtic crosses, perhaps carved from conveniently placed prehistoric standing stones. Over 400 such inscribed stones and crosses survive, mostly in village churchyards. On the death (frequently by gruesome martyrdom) of the saints, churches were often built around the oratories.

The Celtic saints had a rich

variety of names (Breaca, Carantoc, Fimbarrus, Germochus and Meubred to name only five), but for the Saxons and later the Normans they were too unorthodox (not one of them was recognised by Rome) and attempts were made to suppress them. The failure of such attempts is shown in the perpetuation of the saints' names in church and village names. St Nonna's altar became Altarnun; St Ia, St Ives; St Morwenna's oratory, Morwenstow. St Piran's oratory by the sea became Perranporth ('porth' meaning port) and St Winwalloe, who lived in open moorland, gave rise to Gunwalloe, 'gun' or 'goon' being Cornish for moorland.

King Arthur At the time of the 'Coming of the Saints', the darkest period of the Dark Ages, Cornwall was still ruled by its Celtic tribal chiefs, but the pagan Anglo-Saxons were pushing west, threatening the independence of the south-west peninsula. Eventually they were to succeed in conquering all, but their progress was halted by a brilliant Celtic leader for nearly 40 years in the middle of the 6th century. The name that has been given to that leader – still more of a legend than a historical figure – is King Arthur. His Knights of the Round Table were probably the clan warriors or vassals who controlled different parts of the territory.

Unfortunately the association with Tintagel is tenuous. Although there was a monastery here in the 6th c. which Arthur could well have visited, there was no castle until the Normans built one. And without the castle it is difficult to believe that Camelford was really Camelot. But the legend endures. Tintagel

was first suggested as Arthur's home in 1147 by the chronicler Geoffrey of Monmouth, and Cornwall has a stronger identification with Arthur than any of the rival claimants (Brittany, Scotland, Wales and Glastonbury). There are more sites associated with the legend in Cornwall than anywhere else, and right up to the 19th century travellers commented on the local belief that Arthur would return to lead the Cornish forth and out of their miseries.

The Middle Ages After Arthur's death the Anglo-Saxons succeeded in conquering Cornwall, but subsequently left little impact on the landscape. They built few churches, and no new towns. With the arrival of William the Conqueror, however, everything changed. After consolidating his victory at Hastings he gave two-thirds of Cornwall to his half-brother Robert, Count of Mortain, who he made Earl of Cornwall. Although absentee landlords, Robert and his successors made their presence felt with heavy taxes and powerful castles, such as Restormel and Launceston ('Castle Terrible'), to keep the Celts under control. The Normans also rebuilt three-quarters of the county's churches, and today traces of Norman work – some of it very spectacular as at St Germans – are still visible in many of them. It is the fonts which have survived best of all, typically decorated with grotesque faces and semi-geometrical floral patterns.

The 300 years after the Norman Conquest saw the steady growth of Cornwall's population. In 1132 Truro received its charter, and in the 13th century Helston, Lostwithiel, Launceston and Liskeard were incorporated as towns. In 1201 the Stannary Charter established special rights (and taxes) for tin-miners, thus acknowledging their pre-eminence in the Cornish economy. Tin miners were recognised as free-men, owing allegiance to no-one and able to stream for tin as they wished, although their metal had to be stamped and the Stannary tax paid every half-year at one of the four Stannary towns.

In 1337 Edward III made his son, The Black Prince, the first Duke of Cornwall. Since then the sovereign's eldest son has always been the Duke of Cornwall, and the current duke is Prince Charles. Since the time of Henry III none of the dukes has lived in the county, although the Duchy still has huge estates including much of Bodmin Moor and many square miles of land around Restormel Castle.

Rebellion and war In 1485 Henry VII came to the throne, ending the Wars of the Roses. England recognised him as king, but Cornwall did not. A brief rebellion in 1497, in which 200 Cornishmen were brutally killed, was followed a year later by another uprising in support of the pretender Perkin Warbeck. The leaders were all executed. Within 60 years, the Cornish were rebelling again, this time on a religious issue. The Reformation (1536-39) had severed the church from Rome, and throughout most of England the new services in English and the English Prayer Book were brought into use. But in Cornwall the change was received with hostility. To many of the Cornish, English was a language as alien as Latin and the imposition of new services was seen as a threat to traditional Celtic independence. But the uprising

St Germans

of 1549 – this time lacking the support of the gentry who were benefiting from the sale of monastic estates – was easily put down before it got beyond Devon. The end of the Cornish language in churches spelt its death, or rather accelerated it, for it was already disappearing in eastern Cornwall. Cornish survived a little longer but finally expired with its last native speaker in 1777. There are about 400 speakers of Cornish today, but they have learnt the language from textbooks.

In the Civil War Cornwall was one of the most fervently Royalist counties and rallied behind the king, defeating the Parliamentarians in a number of early Royalist victories. Charles I caused a letter of 'Royal Thanks to the People of Cornwall' to be published in every church in the county, and numerous copies of it can still be seen today. In 1644 when the tide was turning, Charles's wife, Queen Henrietta Maria, and Prince Charles (later to return as King Charles II) both stayed in Falmouth before fleeing from England.

Piracy and smuggling One of Charles II's first acts as king was to 'reward' Falmouth for its loyalty with customs and harbour rights. (This was at the expense of Truro, which had supported Cromwell.) More than a symbolic gesture it was recognition of the crucial and growing importance of maritime traffic to Cornwall. Cornwall's earliest trade routes had been by sea, exporting tin to the Mediterranean. Throughout the Middle Ages Cornish ports were amongst the busiest in England, though not the most peaceful. There was no standing navy and wealthy ship-

owners were licensed as privateers. The 'Fowey Gallants' were the most notorious, attacking, boarding and pillaging French and Spanish shipping. The French retaliated, burning Fowey to the ground in 1378, again in 1457, and Looe in 1405. And the Spanish, seeking revenge for the defeat of their Armada in 1588 by a fleet largely manned by men from Devon and Cornwall, sacked Mousehole, Newlyn and Penzance in 1595. Unfortunately the privateers (or pirates as their enemies called them) did not confine themselves to foreign shipping but occasionally attacked the Cinque Ports in Kent and Sussex.

With the development of an English standing navy to patrol the seas, privateering came to an end. But the 18th century saw an alternative method of making a living from the sea: 'fair trading'. Smuggling was not new, but the absence of a militia, the high tariffs on spirits, luxuries and even essentials like salt, along with the complicity of complete neighbourhoods, made it an increasingly popular occupation.

In many villages, such as Polperro, smuggling was the major source of income and special cellars were constructed under the houses for the storage of contraband.

Wrecking Another maritime activity that reached its peak in the 18th century was wrecking. There appears to be little substance to the tales of wreckers who deliberately lured shipping onto the rocks with false lights. The story of the parson who prayed 'not that shipping shall be wrecked, but that if it is, it shall be in this parish' is probably apocryphal, but any ship washed up on the rocks was certain to be plundered. The treacherous cliffs of Cornwall's north coast, and the terrible rocks around Land's End and the Lizard, have always taken a heavy toll of shipping. When a ship was seen in trouble near land, large crowds, armed with ropes, hatchets, axes and crowbars would follow it along the shore, and as reported in the *Penzance Gazette* in 1751 when a ship named *The Endeavour* was finally impaled on rocks 'the whole country poured in, as well reputable farmers and tradesmen as well as the poor and in defiance of the officers loaded horses and even carts with their plunder.' The building of lighthouses and the efficient work of the coastguard lookouts reduced the toll of wrecks, and the stronger enforcement of the law brought wrecking to an end.

Fishing No-one lived by wrecking, but thousands of families were dependent on fishing. Until this century there was not a single coastal village without a few fishing boats. The most important fish was the pilchard, seen in vast shoals off Cornish coasts between July and August each year. The arrival of the shoals, which changed the colour of the water, was observed by the 'huer' or lookout man, who would warn the villagers with a special cry. The fishing boats would then sail out, each trailing part of the seine-net to entrap the shoal. The net was dragged back to shore and the fish unloaded into buckets to be salted, pressed, packed and sold. The quantities were enormous: throughout the 19th century more that 100 million pilchards were caught each year. In one hour in 1834, the seine-fishers of St Ives caught 30 million. They were exported to many different parts of the world, but especially to the Catholic countries to eat on Fridays. Mackerel, herring, and to a lesser extent bass, mullet and hake were also caught. But quite suddenly, at the beginning of this century, the pilchards stopped coming and the fishing industry collapsed. Within a few years hundreds of inshore fishing boats were laid up and canneries closed.

Today the Cornish fishing industry is a shadow of its former self. Only Newlyn has a sizeable inshore, and small off-shore fleet, and Padstow a lobster and crayfish catch which is shipped to Roscoff for the French market. In villages like Mevagissey, Mousehole and St Ives, where the harbours were once filled with fishermen waiting to unload their catches, there are now dinghies, yachts and pleasure craft. Instead of commercial fishing there is shark hunting, and boats offering trips along the coast.

Tin mining and china clay Until about the mid-16th century all mining for tin was on the surface, first by streaming in rivers and later by quarrying along the lodes or seams of ore. From then on mines were underground. But it was not until the end of the 18th century, when the Cornish engineer Richard Trevithick developed a steam engine for pumping out ground water, that shafts of any depth could be sunk. The great gaunt engine houses, now derelict ruins scattered around Bodmin Moor, Penwith and the Camborne area, all once housed beam engines – designed on

Trevithick's principles – for raising ore and water. The deepest mines, setting world records in their time, were as much as 2000 ft below ground (one, the great Dolcoath mine, went down to 3000ft). In other mines, as at Botallack, the men worked directly beneath the sea bed, and could hear the continual din of crashing waves and grinding rocks overhead. Men and boys worked down the mines, in such appalling conditions that they had the shortest life expectancy in the country, worse even than coal miners. Women and children did some of the surface work.

The miners or 'tinners' as they were known had a reputation for 'roughness' which meant drunkenness, violence and lawlessness. It was to these men that the great evangelist John Wesley preached, converting them to Methodism in their thousands on his repeated visits to Cornwall between 1743-89. The church was for the gentry, and since the Prayer Book Rebellion (see above) had had little impact on anybody else. Wesley spoke to the workmen, tinners, fishermen and farmworkers with extraordinary effect, often in mass meetings, as for example at Gwennap where he addressed crowds of 20,000. Simple chapels sprang up all over the county, particularly in the mining villages. Cornwall became a stronghold of Methodism and non-conformity and has remained so, though to a lesser extent, to the present day.

In addition to tin there was mining of lead, iron, zinc, wolfram and most of all, copper. In fact, the copper output of the early 19th century

Cornish tin mine

exceeded that of tin and the Duchy produced two-thirds of the world's copper supply. But then, by the turn of the century, the tin and copper mining, like the fishing, came to a virtual end. The discovery and exploitation of Malaysian tin and African copper flooded the market and the less productive Cornish mines could not compete. Hundreds closed down and the underground shafts quickly flooded with water as the pumping engines stopped. The tinners, unable to find work in Cornwall, emigrated in their thousands to Canada, South Africa and the USA where they continued to work in mines.

Today the high international price of tin has led to the re-opening of four mines, and there are schemes for more ambitious projects. One tin streaming works (at Tolgus) survives and is open to the public, as is the Geevor mine at Pendeen.

Mining may have all but ended, but quarrying – of china clay – is now undertaken on a vast scale and constitutes one of Cornwall's most important industries. The use of china clay for making high quality porcelain was discovered by William Cookworthy late in the 18th century, and was extracted in small quantities by the firm of Josiah Wedgwood north of St Austell. Today a vast expanse of land is covered in huge conical spoil heaps and deep open pits. This weird lunar landscape is caused by the demand for china clay, not only for making pottery but also medicines, toothpaste, cosmetics, shiny 'art-paper' and hundreds of other everyday uses. China clay or kaolin is one of the most important raw materials of modern industry.

20th-century Cornwall It was tourism which saved the economy of the Duchy from total collapse when fishing and mining simultaneously died. 1859 is often considered a watershed for Cornwall, for in that year Brunel's Prince Albert Bridge crossed the River Tamar, bringing the railway to Cornwall. The same year, the first popular guide was published to the county. It advised travellers to allow nine weeks for their holiday because, it said, roads were so bad that it was pleasanter to walk or go on horseback, having one's luggage sent on ahead. But roads rapidly improved and branch railway lines (many now closed) were built to every little town. The late-Victorian passion for sea-bathing brought the first regular visitors. Hotels and boarding houses were built and more followed. Artists came to paint the landscape and colonies of them grew up in picturesque places like St Ives, Newlyn and Lamorna.

But it was not until the age of the motor car and paid holidays that the Cornish tourist industry – like that of its neighbour Devon – got under way. Today Cornwall in summer can be very crowded, with 25-mile traffic jams at the beginning of the summer holiday. Tourism has brought many jobs and new life to the Duchy, but much of the benefit is only seasonal, and it is still quiet for most of the year. It has also brought unsightly development and large caravan sites. On the whole however, building has been discreet, and through careful planning and the work of the National Trust, Cornwall remains one of the most beautiful and unspoilt parts of Britain.

The Best of the Region

A summary of the places of interest in the region, open to the public. The location, with map reference, and description of each place, is shown in the Gazetteer. Names in bold are Gazetteer entries, and those with an asterisk are considered to be of outstanding interest. (NT) indicates properties owned by the National Trust

St Just-in-Roseland church

Churches

Those listed here are specially worth a visit, either for the building itself, or for some special feature such as brasses, heraldry, tomb or wall-painting.

*Altarnun St Nonna

*Blisland SS Protus and Hyacinth

Bodmin St Petroc

Breage St Breaca

Cardinham St Meubred

Crantock St Carantoc

Fowey St Fimbarrus

Kilkhampton St James

*Launcells St Andrew

*Launceston St Mary Magdalene

Lostwithiel St Bartholomew

Morwenstow St Morwenna

Mousehole (Paul) St Pol de Leon

Mullion (Gunwalloe) St Winwallo

Padstow St Petroc

*Porthcurno St Levan

Poughill St Olaf

Probus St Probus

St Austell Holy Trinity

St Buryan St Buryan

St Cleer St Cleer

St Columb Major St Columba

*St Germans St Germans

St Ives St Ia

St Juliot St Juliot

St Kew St Kewa

*St Neot St Neot

Sancreed St Creda

Sennen St Senan

Stratton St Andrew

Tintagel St Merteriana

*Truro Cathedral

Warleggan St Bartholomew

THE BEST OF THE REGION

Historic Houses

Admission to most historic houses is between £1-2 (children half-price)

Antony House (NT)
Apr-Oct, Tue-Thur & Bank Hol Mon 2-6

*Cotehele (NT)
Apr-Oct, daily 11-6; Nov-Mar gardens only, daily 9-dusk

Godolphin House
May-Jun, Thur 2-5; Jul-Sep, Tue & Thur 2-5

*Lanhydrock House (NT)
Apr-Oct, daily 11-6; Nov-Mar gardens only, daily 9-dusk

Mount Edgcumbe
House: May-Sep, Mon & Tue 2-6
Park and gardens: all year daily 10-6

Newquay Trerice (NT)
Apr-Oct, daily 11-6

Padstow Abbey House
Open at owner's discretion during summer

Pencarrow House
Easter-Sep, Tue-Fri & Sun 1.30-5.30 (opens 11am Bank Hol Mon & Jun-Aug). Gardens: Easter-Sep daily

Probus Trewithen
House: Apr-Jul, Mon-Tue 2-4.30
Gardens: Mar-Sep, weekdays 2-4.30

*St Michael's Mount (NT)
Nov-Mar, Mon, Wed & Fri conducted tours of house at 11, 12, 2, 3, 4 (weather & tide permitting); Apr-May, Mon, Wed & Fri 10.30-5.45 (last admission 4.45); Jun-Oct, Mon-Wed & Fri 10.30-5.45 (last admission 4.45). (NB: Ferry only operates in the summer months, otherwise access is only possible at low tide)

Tintagel Old Post Office (NT)
Apr-Oct, daily 11-6 or sunset if earlier

Trelowarren
Easter Mon, May Bank Hol, Jun-Jul, Wed & Sun; Aug-mid Sep, Tue, Wed & Sun; mid Sep-end Oct, Wed 2.30-5

Trewint Cottage
All year daily 9.30-6

Parks, Gardens & Wildlife

Admission to the gardens of historic houses is usually included in a combined ticket for house and garden. (See admission to historic houses above.) Where the garden can be visited separately this is usually about half the price of the combined ticket. The entrance fee for other gardens open to the public is usually in the range 30-50p (Children half-price or less).

*Cotehele (NT)
House & garden. See *Historic Houses*

Fowey Aquarium
Easter-Sep, daily 10-5

*Glendurgan Gardens (NT)
Mar-Oct, Mon, Wed & Fri (closed Good Fri) 10.30-4.30

Gweek Cornish Seal Sanctuary
Easter-Oct, daily 9.30-7; Nov-Mar, daily 10-5

Hayle Bird Paradise
See *Leisure Parks & Model Railways*

Kilkhampton Coombe Valley Nature Trail
Daily, all year

Lanhydrock House (NT)
House & garden. See *Historic Houses*

Looe Monkey Sanctuary
Easter, May-Sep, Sun-Fri 10.30-6

Mevagissey Aquarium
May-Oct, daily 10-dusk

*Mount Edgcumbe
House & park. See *Historic Houses*

Newquay Aquarium
Spring Bank Hol-mid Oct, daily 10-dusk

Newquay Dairyland and Country Life Museum
See *Industrial & Rural Heritage*

Newquay Trerice (NT)
House and garden. See *Historic Houses*

Newquay Leisure Park and Zoo
See *Leisure Parks & Model Railways*

Padstow Tropical Bird and Butterfly Gardens
Summer, daily 10.30-8; winter, daily 10.30-5

Pencarrow House
House & garden. See *Historic Houses*

Penzance Morrab Gardens
Daily, all year

***Probus** County Demonstration
Gardens
Oct-Apr, Mon-Fri 10-4.30; May-Sep
Mon-Fri 10-5, Sun 2-6

Probus Trewithen
House & garden. See *Historic Houses*

Ruan Minor Poltesco-Cadgwith
Nature Trail
Daily, all year

St Tudy Bear Oak Gardens
Jun-Sep, Mon-Fri 11.30-5

***Trelissick Gardens** (NT)
Apr-Oct, Mon-Sat 11-6, Sun 1-6

***Trengwainton Gardens** (NT)
Mar-Oct, Wed-Sat & Bank Hol 11-6

Castle, Ruins & Ancient Sites

Unless otherwise stated, these sites are
accessible at all reasonable times.

Blisland Stripple Stones, Trippet
Stones
Bronze Age stone circles

Callington Dupath Well
Ancient holy well

Cardinham Bury Castle
Iron Age hill fort

***Chysauster** Ancient British village
Mar 15-Oct 15, Mon-Sat 9.30-6.30,
Sun 2-6.30; Oct 16-Mar 14, Mon-Sat
9.30-4, Sun 2-4

Constantine Pixies' Hall
Prehistoric underground passage

***Falmouth** Pendennis Castle
Times as for Chysauster

Fowey St Catherine's Castle

Golant Castle Dore
Prehistoric earthwork

Lamorna Two Pipers, sarsen stones;
Merry Maidens, complete stone circle;
Tregiffian Barrow, Bronze Age tomb

***Launceston** Castle
Times as for Chysauster

Lelant Trencrom
Iron Age hill fort

***Lostwithiel** Restormel Castle
Times as for Chysauster

***Madron** Chun Castle, Iron Age hill
fort; Chun Quoit, megalithic chamber
tomb; Lanyon Quoit, megalithic
chamber tomb; Men-an-Tol, standing
stones

Perranporth Oratory of St Piran

***Roche** St Michael's Chapel
Ruined medieval hermit's chapel

St Breward King Arthur's Hall
Prehistoric enclosure

***St Cleer** The Hurlers, group of stone
circles; King Doniert's Stone,
monolith; Trethevy Quoit, megalithic
chamber tomb

St Clether Holy well

St Columb Major Nine Maidens, row
of standing stones; Castle-an-Dinas,
Iron Age hill fort

St Keyne Holy well

***St Mawes** Castle
Times as for Chysauster

Sancreed Carn Euny, Ancient British
village; Caer Bran, Iron Age hill fort

***Tintagel** Castle
Times as for Chysauster

Wadebridge Medieval bridge

Warbstow Bury
Prehistoric fort

***Zennor** Zennor Quoit
Megalithic chamber tomb

Museums & Galleries

Bodmin Museum of the Duke of
Cornwall's Light Infantry
Apr-Feb, Mon-Fri 9-12.30 & 2-4.45,
closed Bank Hols

Bude Historical and Folk Exhibition
May-Sep, daily 12-4 (10-6 in high
season)

Bude Militaria Museum
May-Sep, daily 10-6

Camborne School of Mines Museum
See *Industrial & Rural Heritage*

Camborne Shire Horse and Carriage
Museum
See *Industrial & Rural Heritage*

Camelford North Cornwall Museum
and Gallery
See *Industrial & Rural Heritage*

Cotehele National Maritime Museum
Gallery
See *Historic Houses*

Dobwalls Thorburn Museum and Art
Gallery
Apr-Sep, daily 10-6; Oct, Wed & Sun
10-4.30

Fowey Noah's Ark Folk Museum
Mon-Sat 10-4, closes at 12 Wed & Sat

Fowey Town Museum
Easter, May-Sep, Mon-Fri 9.30-12.30
& 2.30-4.30

Helston Museum
Mon-Sat 10.30-12.30 & 2-4.30, closed
Wed afternoon

Launceston Lawrence House Museum
Apr-Sep, Mon-Fri (closed Bank Hols)
10.30-12.30 & 2.30-4.30

Looe Guildhall Museum
Apr-Sep, Mon-Fri 10-6, Sun 2-4

Lostwithiel Town Museum
Mid May-Sep, Mon-Fri 10.15-12.30 &
2-4.30; closed Wed afternoon

Newlyn Art Gallery
Open for special exhibitions only:
Mon-Sat 10-5

Newquay Trenance Museum
Spring Bank Hol-Sep, daily 10-8

Penzance Penlee House Museum
Mon-Fri 12.30-4.30

Penzance Nautical Museum
May-Sep, weekdays 10-1 & 2-4

Penzance Royal Geological Society of
Cornwall Museum
Easter-Sep, Mon-Fri 2-5

Polperro Museum of Smuggling
Easter-Sep, daily 10-7

*St Austell Charlestown Shipwreck
Museum
Apr-Sep, daily 10-6 (dusk in summer)

St Ives Barbara Hepworth Museum
and Sculpture Garden
Oct-Mar, Mon-Sat 10-4.30; Apr-Jun &
Sep, Mon-Sat 10-5.30; Jul & Aug,
Mon-Sat 10-6.30, Sun 2-6

St Ives Barnes Museum of
Cinematography
Mon-Sat 11-1 & 2.30-5

St Ives Penwith Art Gallery
Tue-Sat 10-1 & 2.30-5

St Keyne Paul Corin Musical
Collection
Easter week, May-Sep, daily 10.30-1 &
2.30-5

St Stephen Automobilia Museum
Summer, daily 10-7; winter daily, but
ring for entry

*Truro County Museum & Art Gallery
Mon-Sat (not Bank Hols) 9-1 & 2-5.
Closed Mon, Oct-Easter

Wheal Martyn Museum
See *Industrial and Rural Heritage*

Zennor Folk Museum
See *Industrial & Rural Heritage*

Industrial & Rural Heritage

*Botallack Old tin mines

Bude Canal

Calstock Viaduct

*Camborne Cornish Engines (NT)
Apr-Oct, daily 11-6

Camborne School of Mines Museum
Mon-Fri 9-4.30, closed Bank Hols

Camborne Shire Horse and Carriage
Museum
Easter-Sep, daily 10-6

*Camelford North Cornwall Museum
and Gallery
Apr-Sep, Mon-Sat 10.30-5

Cotehele Quay, Tamar Sailing Barge
See *Historic Houses*

*Delabole Slate quarry
Apr-Sep, daily 10-5 (last tour 4)

Newquay Dairyland and Country Life
Museum
Mid Mar-early Nov, daily 1.30-5;
Easter week & May-Sep, 10-5; milking
3.15-4.30

Newquay Huer's Hut

Pendeen Geevor Mine
Apr-Oct, daily 10-5.30

*****Redruth** Tolgus Tin Mill
Late Apr-Sep, daily 10-6

Redruth Viaduct

St Agnes Wheal Coates Engine House

St Neot Carnglaze Slate Caverns
Easter-Sep, Sun-Fri 2-5; Bank Hols &
Jul-Aug, Mon-Fri 10.30-5, Sun 2-5

Saltash Prince Albert Bridge

Wendron Poldark Mine
Apr-Oct, daily 10-6

*****Wheal Martyn** China Clay Open Air
Museum
Apr-Oct, daily 10-6

Zennor Folk Museum
May-Sep, daily 10-5

Natural Features

*****Bedruthan Steps** N coast bay

*****Bodmin Moor** Brown Willy, highest
point in Cornwall; Rough Tor, second
highest point

*****Boscastle** N coast fjord with
blowholes

Bude Widemouth Bay, N coast beach

Cadgwith Devil's Frying Pan, S coast
punch-bowl

Carn Brea Prominent inland hill

Cubert Holywell Bay, N coast

*****Dozmary Pool** Bodmin Moor

Gwennap Pit, amphitheatre caused by
mining subsidence

Gwithian Hell's Mouth, N coast
foreland

Harlyn Bay, N coast

Kilkhampton Coombe valley, N coast

*****Kynance Cove**, S coast

Lamorna Cove, S coast

*****Land's End**

Lizard Point Furthest S point in
Britain

*****Mullion Cove** S coast

*****Newquay** Beaches, N coast

Perranporth Penhale Sands, N coast

Porthcurno Bay on S coast

*****Porthleven** The Loe, freshwater lake
on S coast

Prussia Cove S coast

*****St Cleer** The Cheesewring, Bodmin
Moor Tor

St Michael's Mount
See *Historic Houses*

Zennor Gurnard's Head, N coast

Leisure Parks & Model Railways

Carn Brea Leisure Centre
All year, Mon-Fri 9-10.30pm,
weekends 9-5.30

Dobwalls Forest Railroad Park
Apr-Sep, daily 10-6; Oct, Wed & Sun
10-4.30

Hayle Gwinear Outdoor Model
Railway
Easter-Sep, daily 10-dusk

Hayle Paradise Park and Bird
Sanctuary
Daily all year, 10-1 hr before sunset;
miniature railway Easter-mid Sep,
daily 11-5

Hayle Towans Passenger Carrying
Miniature Railway
Spring Bank Hol-Sep, daily 10-8

Helston Aero Park and Flambards
Village
Easter-Oct, daily 10-5

Lelant Model Village
Easter-Oct daily 10-5; high season 10-10

Marazion World of Entertainment
Easter-mid Oct, Mon-Fri 10-5.30, Sun
2.30-5.30

Mevagissey Model Railway
Easter-Sep, daily 11-6; winter Suns
only 2-5

Newquay Lappa Valley Railway
Apr-Sep, daily 11-5, high season 10-6,
Oct Suns only 11-5

Newquay Leisure Park and Zoo
All year, daily 10-dusk

Polperro Land of Legend and Model Village
Mid Mar-Oct, 10.30-6.30; high season 10.30-9.30

St Agnes Leisure Park
Mid Mar-mid Oct, daily 9.30-10pm

St Austell Carlyon Bay Cornish Leisure World
Beaches, mini-golf etc. Summer, daily 9-dusk; disco: every evening, winter Wed-Sat; Coliseum auditorium: events advertised locally

Famous Connections

Many famous – or simply unusual – personalities have been connected with Cornwall throughout its history. Details of their association will be found under the Gazetteer entries.

Charles I Golant (Castle Dore)

Charles II Cotehele, Falmouth (Pendennis Castle)

Davy, Sir Humphrey Penzance

Drake, Sir Francis Bossiney

du Maurier, Daphne Bolventor, Fowey

George III Cotehele

Grahame, Kenneth Fowey

Hardy, Thomas St Juliot

Hawker, Rev Robert Morwenstow

Henrietta Maria, Queen Falmouth (Pendennis Castle)

Hepworth, Barbara St Ives

Lawrence, D.H. Zennor

Leach, Bernard St Ives

Murdock, William Redruth

Pentreath, Dolly Mousehole

Quiller-Couch, Sir Arthur Fowey

Raleigh, Sir Walter Padstow, Falmouth

Trevithick, Richard Camborne

Wesley, John Gwennap, St Just, Trewint Cottage

Arthurian Cornwall

The sites listed below associated with King Arthur are supposition, but the location of so many in such a small area of Cornwall gives substance to the legend. See also p.10.

Bossiney Site of the Round Table

Camelford The original Camelot

Camelford *Slaughter Bridge* Site of Arthur's fatal last battle

Dozmary Pool Excalibur returned here on Arthur's death

Golant *Castle Dore* Home of King Mark, Tristram and Isolde; Arthur and the Knights were entertained here

St Breward *King Arthur's Hall*

St Columb Major *Castle-an-Dinas* The Knights' hunting lodge

Tintagel *Castle* Arthur's birthplace and centre of the Arthurian legend

Tintagel *Merlin's Cave* Watery home of the magician

Warbstow Bury Arthur's burial place

Hotels & Historic Inns

† Non-residential inn
(THF) A Trusthouse Forte Hotel

Bolventor
Jamaica Inn
Bolventor PL15 7TS
Tel (056686) 250
Built in 1547 on bleakest Bodmin Moor, the inn owes its fame to Daphne du Maurier's novel. Named after the rum traffic, it came under the influence of local Methodism in the late 19th c. and until the 1940s was a temperance hostel. For a while it was owned by the novelist Alistair Maclean.

Bude
Strand Hotel (THF)
The Strand, Bude EX23 8RA
Tel (0288) 3222
Built in the late 1960s and extended later, this 40-room holiday hotel stands on the banks of the River Neet and is a short walk from the main shopping centre and the sandy beaches.

Fowey
The King of Prussia
Town Quay, Fowey PL23 1AT
Tel (072683) 2450

One of the grandest buildings in Fowey, (much bigger than the Town Hall) with a fine granite portico, the inn was once owned by John Carter, Cornwall's most notorious smuggler, and is named after his boyhood hero. He used to have a battery of cannons to protect his private landing-beach, and the pub was an important outlet for his contraband drink. Wide choice of beers.

Helston
The Angel
Coinagehall Street, Helston TR13 8EF
Tel (03265) 2701

An inn in the 15th c., the building became the Godolphin family's town house and later a magistrate's court. It ultimately reverted to being an inn, but the old minstrels' gallery remains in the dining room. Good bar snacks and restaurant.

Launceston
The White Hart
Broad Street, Launceston PL15 8AA
Tel (0566) 3567

A scheduled building of great historic interest in the town's main square. The doorway is all that remains of the original medieval priory. The rest of the building is later, the imposing façade dating from the 18th c. when this was one of Cornwall's most important coaching inns. Good choice of bar food and table d'hôte restaurant.

Lostwithiel
The Royal Oak Inn
Lostwithiel PL22 0AG
Tel (0208) 872552

Built in the 13th c. and basically octagonal in shape, *The Royal Oak* looks more like a castle than an inn. The Black Prince regularly dined here, while the Duke of Cornwall and is said to have constructed a secret passage from the building to Restormel Castle. King Charles I stayed in 1628. The bars still have the original stone floors and stained glass windows. Wide choice of real ales; separate restaurant.

Morwenstow
†*The Bush Inn*
Morwenstow, Bude EX23 9FR
Tel (028883) 242

Reputed to be over 1000 years old, the inn retains a piscina which suggests that a part of it was a chapel in the 13th c. Later, because of its remote position in N Cornwall, it was used by smugglers. Very welcoming.

Padstow
The Golden Lion Hotel
Lanadwell Street, Padstow PL28 8AN
Tel (0841) 532797

The 'Hobby Horse' of Padstow's famous May festival lives in this 16th-c. inn, built of granite blocks with a slate roof. Until last century it was a meeting place for wreckers who would barter and sell their booty here. Excellent 'ploughman's' at the bar.

Metropole Hotel (THF)
Station Road, Padstow PL28 8DB
Tel (0841) 532486

This hotel's friendly, informal atmosphere makes it ideal for the family holiday. Situated close to the harbour, it has panoramic views across the sands of the Camel Estuary. Heated outdoor swimming pool.

St Breward
†*The Old Inn*
St Breward, Bodmin PL30 4PP
Tel (0208) 850711

Next to the church, this popular pub for moorland walkers is in parts 700 years old. It is built entirely of whitewashed rough granite with a rag slate roof. Basket meals, bar snacks and mead available.

Sennen
†*The First and Last Inn*
Sennen, Land's End, Penzance TR19 7AR
Tel (073687) 680

Less than 1m from Land's End, this was for 650 years the last mainland hostelry this side of the Atlantic. Once used by the smugglers and wreckers of Sennen Cove as a staging post for moving goods E, the inn has been popular with visitors to Land's End since Dr Johnson and Lord Nelson both came here 200 years ago. Free house with mead, cider and real ale.

Sports & Recreation

Boating and sailing The S coast of Cornwall is a sailing and boating paradise, the placid estuaries of the Fowey and Helford being particularly suitable. Many of the resorts have their own sailing clubs: the main centre on the Cornish Riviera is Falmouth, which has a regatta in August. For those who prefer someone else 'to do the driving' there are excellent boat trips from fishing villages such as Polperro and Mevagissey, and from all the main resorts. Another good trip is by river from Truro down the Fal to the coast at Falmouth. The N coast has good sailing on the Camel estuary with clubs at Padstow, Rock and Wadebridge.

Fishing There is game fishing on the Camel, Fowey and Tamar, and the Siblyback Reservoir on Bodmin Moor is well stocked with rainbow and brown trout. Boats can be hired for sea-fishing at many of the fishing ports, and deep-water anglers can be taken out to the numerous wrecks where the really big fish lurk. Shark-fishing has become very popular on the S coast, with Looe the main centre. For further information on freshwater fishing contact the South-West Water Authority, 3-5 Barnfield Road, Exeter Tel (0392) 31666

Golf There are a large number of golf clubs, most of which welcome non-members. Most of them are seaside courses, with St Enodoc course at Rock being particularly enchanting.

Riding Hacking, hunting and pony-trekking are available throughout the region. Pony-trekking is concentrated on Bodmin Moor, with many stables offering full tuition and all the necessary equipment.

Surfing There is no question that Cornwall is the best area of Britain for surfing, with excellent beaches at St Ives, Newquay, Perranporth and Bude. Conditions on the sheltered Camel estuary at Rock are ideal for the new sport of wind-surfing.

Festivals & Events

February *St Columb Major* Hurling Competition (Shrove Tue & next Sat)

March *Falmouth* Spring Flower Show (late Mar); *Penzance* West Cornwall Spring Show (late Mar)

May *Padstow* Hobby Horse Celebration (May 1); *Saltash* Fair Weekend (1st week); *Helston* Furry Dance (May 8); *Gwennap* Annual Methodist Gathering (Spring Bank Hol Mon); *Newquay* Carnival Week (last week and 1st week in Jun)

June *Wadebridge* Royal Cornwall Show (mid-month); *Launceston* Agricultural Show (2nd or 3rd week); *Liskeard* Carnival Week (3rd week); *Saltash* Regatta (3rd week); *Penzance* Eve of Sts Peter and John (Jun 28); *Warleggan* Carnival (last week)

July *St Germans* Elephant Fayre (last weekend)

August *Bude* Blessing of the Sea (dependent on tides); *Mousehole* Carnival (1st or 2nd week); *Falmouth* Regatta Week (mid-month); *Fowey* Royal Regatta and Carnival Week (2nd or 3rd week); *Bude* Carnival and Fete (3rd week); *Penryn* Town Fair (Bank Hol weekend)

September *Helston* Harvest Fair (1st week); *Looe* International Sea Angling Festival (3rd week); *St Ives* Music and Arts Festival

October *Callington* Honey Fair (1st week)

November *Liskeard* Fat Stock Show (2nd week)

Walks

There are unlimited numbers of beautiful walks in Cornwall, and the 10 listed below are simply a selection in some of the most beautiful and unspoilt parts of the county. All are circular and can be undertaken without difficulty in a day. However none should be attempted without the relevant 1:50,000 OS map and a good pair of boots.

The entire coastline is now open to walkers, and every stretch of it is rewarding (see below). Shorter walks from the major resorts are described under the relevant Gazetteer entries.

Cornwall Coast Path

All Cornwall's magnificent coastline can now be covered by foot along the Cornwall Coast Path. These 268 miles form the central part of the South West Way which runs along the coast from Minehead in N Somerset to Poole Harbour in Dorset, which at 523 miles is the longest continuous path in the country.

One major attraction of the path is its enormous variety: inland the views vary from moorland to rich arable farmland, and the coastline is never the same. The N stretch from the Devon border to Padstow has wild scenery with sheer cliff faces and few accessible beaches. From Padstow to St Ives there are still fabulous stretches of cliff walking but also sandy bays and fine beaches; some are very crowded in summer, others accessible only to the walker. On the S coast the scenery is generally gentler with the exception of the Lizard peninsula. There are beautiful sheltered bays and estuaries not found on the N coast.

The entire path is waymarked with signposts with either 'Cornwall Coast Path', 'S.W.C.P.'. or the symbol of an acorn. However, not all the walking is easy. Some stretches are relatively flat, but others involve steep climbs and even scree walking. No-one should undertake the sections Tintagel-Port Isaac and St Ives-Pendeen Watch without sturdy boots and reasonable experience.

A number of detailed guides are published for the long-distance walker. The best is the guide published annually by the *South West Way Association* (1982 edn 90p) obtainable in some bookshops or from P. H. Carter, Beaver Lodge, Rundle Road, Newton Abbot, Devon. The HMSO official guide *The Cornwall Coast Path* by Edward Byatt (£3.95) is also good. Penguin Books are about to produce a guide to the path as well. Seven circular walks involving some of the best sections of the path are described.

Walk 1 *N Coast: Coombe & Morwenstow*   1C
Leave Kilkhampton W by car and park in Coombe. Walk W down road to the sea. Follow coast path N past Lower Sharpnose Point to Stanbury Mouth. Here leave the coast and walk inland along footpath (which joins a track but leaves it again when the track turns left) to Eastaway on the minor road. Cross the road and continue to Woodford on footpath. From here take track S into wood. The track ends in the wood but cross the stream to join footpath on S side of stream. Follow it back (it becomes a track after ½m) into Coombe. This walk can be extended by walking on along the coast from Stanbury Mouth past Higher Sharpnose Point, past the gully where the River Tidna enters the sea to Vicarage Cliff. From here take footpath E into Morwenstow. A footpath from the inn leads S to Stanbury and Eastaway. From Eastaway return as in the shorter walk. 5m/8m

Walk 2 *N Coast: Pentire Point*   2B
Park in Polzeath or New Polzeath. Walk N along the coast path to Pentire Point; on W to Rumps Point. Continue S along coast path past Com Head and then take path due S to Pentireglaze. Just after the farm take footpath W back to Polzeath/4m

Walk 3 *Land's End – Porthcurno*   4C
Park in Land's End Car Park. Follow Cornwall Coast Path S to Gwennap Head and on to St Levan. Go inland to St Levan Church. Cross stream and go on footpath to Ardensawah Farm. From here follow footpath straight on NW to Bosistow and on to Trevilley. From here follow short track to B3315. Turn left and continue to the A30. It is ¾m to the car park/8m

Walk 4 *S Coast: The Loe*   4A
Park in Helston. Walk out on B3304 (signposted Porthleven). Cross River Loe and then in 50 yds take track left along river estuary. Follow it, keeping the Loe on your left, through Penrose to Loe Bar and the sea (3½m). Walk SE along Loe Bar and return via Carminowe Creek and E bank of the Loe/7m

Walk 5 *S Coast: Lizard Point* 4A
Park in Cadgwith car park. Walk down
to sea and S along the Cornwall Coast
Path to Lizard Point and on to Kynance
Cove. There walk up Landrover track
from tea hut for 200yds (around
hairpin bend) and then take old track
to the NE. In 2m this crosses the A3083
– cross it and continue to minor road
(another ½m). Turn right and in ¾m
left. Return via road to car park/8m

Walk 6 *S Coast: Fowey* 3C
Park in Fowey. Walk S along main
street to jetty and take ferry to
Polruan. Walk up hill a short distance
and take first turning on the right.
Take signposted footpath to Bodinnick
and walk along top of wood to road.
Continue along road to head of Pont
Pill Creek. Cross river and take
turning left back down the other side
of creek. Immediately take footpath
signposted 'Hall Walk'. Follow it along
creek wood past the Quiller-Couch
monument and N into Bodinnick.
Take ferry back to Fowey/4½m

Walk 7 *S Coast: Plymouth Sound* 3D
Park in Cremyll. Walk S along coast
path through Mount Edgcumbe Park
to Kingsand. Walk back uphill
through village and along road back to
Cremyll for 1m. Take track on right
just before B3247 and in 100yds take
footpath (left) towards church. Just
before church cross the road and take
footpath for Empacombe and Cremyll.
This walk can be substantially
lengthened by continuing along the
coast from Kingsand, through
Cawsand to Penlee Point and Rame
Head. From here continue along coast
path until it joins the road (1½m). In
¼m take path right leading NE to
Treninnow. If you miss the path, take
the track 100yds further on. Just
beyond Treninnow Farm at the
intersection take the left fork into
Millbrook. Walk through village and
join minor road E along Millbrook
Lake. After 2½m take footpath (left)
back to Cremyll/7m/12m

Walk 8 *Carn Brea* 3A
Park in Carnkie S of Carn Brea. Walk
up track to top of Carn Brea. At top
walk W along path at top of scarp and
down to Penhallick. At the road turn

left and in 200yds leave it by turning
right down footpath (and downhill) to
road. Cross road and when path
diverges in 200yds take left fork and
join track going uphill to Carn Arthen.
At road turn right. At T-junction turn
left and continue down road to 2nd
left. Take it and in 100yds take
footpath E to Treskillard. In village go
straight on down road 100yds and then
take track right going E past disused
mines. At road turn left and walk back
into Carnkie/4½m

Walk 9 *N Bodmin Moor: Highest
Cornwall* 2C
From Camelford N on A39 take first
right for Rough Tor. Park at end of
road. Walk up path to the top of
Rough Tor. From here walk SE to
Brown Willy (1½m – no path). Walk
W down Brown Willy to reach
Fernacre Farm (1m) on the opposite
side of the stream. Go ½m along path
W (past stone circle on right) to bridge
over small stream. There turn N (no
path) keeping Rough Tor on your right
and Louden Hill on your left. From
the saddle walk down the stream (still
going N) back to your car. (NB Not
recommended in misty weather.)/6m

Walk 10 *S Bodmin Moor: The
Cheesewring* 2C
Park in Minions. Take either of the old
miners' tracks N and climb up to the
Cheesewring. Climb to the top of
Stowe's Hill (The Cheesewring is on its
S face) and from there strike N (no
path) to Sharptor. When you meet the
track going W, follow it to the farm
and ½m further to where it divides.
Take the left fork to the ruin. From
here go ½m W to the track running
NS and follow it S to Siblyback. From
here take the left fork which goes S
down the valley 1m until it meets
another track which comes in on the
left. Follow this track to the Siblyback
Reservoir. Continue round the
reservoir on the track until you meet
the minor road. Keeping to the N of
the stream, strike E (no path) to
Trewalla (1m), and the Hurlers
standing stones (another 1m). From
the Hurlers take the track down to
Minions. (NB Not recommended
without a compass or in mist.)/7½m

Motoring tours

The tours are circular and can be started at any point. A full day should be allowed for each tour, with the exception of No 4, for which half a day should be sufficient. Names in brackets indicate diversions from the main route.

Tour 1 *Newquay, Hayle, Camborne and Padstow*
From Newquay S on A3075 – right at Goonhavern on B3285 to Perranporth – St Agnes – B3277 – after 2m, minor road right to Porthtowan – minor road signposted Redruth and Portreath – after 2m, right fork to B3300 and Portreath – B3301 – Gwithian – Hayle – E on A30 – A3047 to Camborne – (Carn Brea) – Redruth (all of which may be bypassed on A30) – from Redruth E following signposts for A30 and Bodmin – A39 to St Columb Major – (Castle-an-Dinas) – after 3m B3274 to Padstow – B3276 – Trenance – Newquay

Tour 2 *Penwith: Penzance, Land's End and St Ives*
From Penzance W along promenade – Newlyn – Coast road to Mousehole – at harbour turn right, inland to Paul – left at Paul church, after 1m left onto B3315 – (Lamorna) – Merry Maidens stone circle – (Porthcurno) – Land's End – A30 to Sennen – (Sennen Cove) – B3306 to St Just – Botallack – Pendeen – (Lanyon Quoit, signposted Madron) – Zennor – St Ives – return to Penzance via B3311

Tour 3 *Falmouth, Lizard Point and Helston*
From Falmouth N on A39 – left before Penryn on B3291 – Gweek – S and then E on B3293 – (St Keverne, Coverack) – E of Earth Tracking Station take minor road S across Goonhilly Downs – after 3½m, left to Poltesco – follow signs to Ruan Minor – Cadgwith – W to A3083 – left to Lizard town and Lizard Point – back along A3083 for 4m to B3296 – Mullion town – (Mullion Cove) – at Mullion church take minor road to Cury – after 2m rejoin A3083 – NW to Helston – (Porthleven) – NE on A394 to Penryn – A39 back to Falmouth

Bedruthan Steps

Tour 4 *Truro, Tregony and St Mawes*
From Truro E on A39 – A390 – Probus – (Trewithen house and gardens) – at Probus church minor road S to A3078 – E to Tregony – Continue S on A3078 and after 2m left on minor road and follow signs to Portloe – Veryan – rejoin A3078 – SW to Just-in-Roseland – (St Mawes) – B3289 N to King Harry Ferry – Trelissick Gardens – right at A39 and back to Truro

Tour 5 *Liskeard, Looe and Fowey*
From Liskeard S on A38 signposted Plymouth – after 8m B3249 – St Germans – A374 (detour left on A374 and B3247 to Mount Edgcumbe house

and gardens, Kingsand and Cawsand) – left at A387 – Looe – Polperro – W on minor road (very steep) signposted Lansallos and Fowey – after 2m right fork signposted Fowey and Bodinnick – at T-junction right, and in 200yds left – after ¾m right fork, after 2m left to Bodinnick. Ferry to Fowey – B3269 – (Golant) – A390 N to Lostwithiel – (Restormel Castle) – Dobwalls – A38 – Liskeard

Tour 6 *Bodmin Moor*
From Bodmin A30 E for Launceston – after 5m left to Blisland – straight on NW to St Breward – through village and at T-junction in ½m turn left – fork right after river and join B3266 –

N to Camelford – after 4m right on A395 to rejoin A30 – (Launceston) – W on A30 – (Altarnun) – Trewint – Bolventor (Dozmary Pool) – minor road at fork E of Bolventor (signposted St Cleer) 7m S to Redgate crossroads – left for Common Moor – King Doniert's Stone – (St Cleer, Trethevy Quoit) – left fork after Common Moor for Minions (The Hurlers, Cheesewring) – return to Redgate crossroads and continue W for St Neot – (Warleggan) – Mount – Cardinham – at crossroads N of Cardinham church turn left and go W on minor road to A30 and return S to Bodmin

Gazetteer

EC: Early closing MD: Market Day
Populations over 10,000 shown
Map references after place names
refer to map inside back cover

This includes information on the location, history and main features of the places of interest in the region. Visiting hours for all places open to the public are shown in 'The Best of the Region'. Asterisks indicate references to other Gazetteer entries

Launceston Castle

Altarnun   2C
Village on Bodmin Moor off A30, 10m SW of Launceston

Named after 'the altar of St Nonna', the village is famous for its 15th-16th-c. **Church of St Nonna**. Sometimes known as 'the Cathedral of Bodmin Moor', it has a 109ft granite tower, making it one of the tallest in Cornwall. Inside, the church is a fine example of Cornish architecture at its most typical. There are two wide aisles and an impressive 15th-c. barrel roof and, as is common in Cornwall but rare in the rest of England, the splendid Norman font is preserved. Of special interest are the 79 carved bench ends of the instruments of the Passion, a bagpipe player, a fool and a fiddler. One by the font proudly declares the craftsman 'Robert Daye, maker of this worke'; the 16th-c. date in Roman numerals is unfortunately damaged. In the churchyard is a large Celtic cross and the graves of Digory Isbell and his wife Elizabeth who gave hospitality to John Wesley at the nearby *Trewint Cottage when he came to Cornwall to promote Methodism. Below the church, separating it from the village, runs a stream with two bridges, one modern and an ancient one for packhorses.

The village itself is delightful: well-known for its flowers which won a recent Britain-in-Bloom contest.

Antony House (NT)   3D
Historic house nr Torpoint 5m W of Plymouth via Torpoint Ferry

Described as the most distinguished classical house in Cornwall, Antony House was built for Sir William Carew between 1710-21. The plain and dignified central block is of granite and has a carriage porch in front. Its wings are of red brick, connected to the house by arcades.

Inside there are fine panelled rooms, period furniture and a good collection of portraits of the Carew family, owners of the estate since the late 15th c. In the Civil War the family was unhappily divided, some members supporting the king and others Parliament. There is a portrait (crudely stitched together after being cut down from its frame by Royalist Carews) of the Parliamentarian Sir Alexander, executed in 1644. The family, who still live at Antony, gave the house to the National Trust in 1961.

In the extensive grounds (laid out by Humphrey Repton *c*. 1800) is a dovecote contemporary with the house and a bath house of 1748. Also in the park is the Victorian family church.

Bedruthan Steps 2B
Natural feature on N coast off B3276, 6m N of Newquay

Backed by cliffs guarded by the National Trust, this is one of the most spectacular, and most photographed views on Cornwall's rugged N coast. The seas crash against dramatically shaped free-standing rocks – the stepping stones of the legendary giant, Bedruthan – and into the dark caverns below the cliff edge. The beach is reached by 123 steps.

Blisland 2C
Village on Bodmin Moor off A30, 9m NE of Bodmin

Grouped around a lush village green with wide-spaced granite cottages, ivy-covered stone walls and tall trees, Blisland has much of the character of a Yorkshire Dale village. The basically Norman **Church of SS Protus and Hyacinth** has a medieval atmosphere, enhanced rather than reduced by the sensitive restoration (1896-1930) when the highly coloured wooden rood screen was built.

The interior has a charmingly erratic appearance, with the granite columns of the arcades leaning rakishly and the ribs of the barrel roofs distorted. Unusually the church has two fonts, one Norman and an octagonal one of the 15th c. On the N wall of the nave is a painted panel with the royal arms of James I (1604). The granite tower is 15th-c. Also on the village green is a 17th-c. *manor house* and the excellent *Royal Oak* inn.

There are numerous barrows, hut circles and earthworks marking the intense prehistoric activity on this part of Bodmin Moor. The most impressive

are the *Stripple Stones* by Hawks Tor 3m NE. These are the remains of a large Bronze Age stone circle about 145ft in diameter, enclosed within a ditch and bank with a central standing stone of 13ft. The *Trippet Stones* between the Stripple Stones and the village form a smaller circle with 8 standing and 12 fallen stones, 108ft in diameter.

Bodinnick see *Fowey*

Bodmin 2C
Pop 12,300. 12m N of St Austell (A391). EC Wed, MD Sat.

The county town of Cornwall, Bodmin makes a good base for visitors. It is only 12m from the N and S coasts and is on the edge of the beautiful Bodmin Moor.

The Celtic hermit St Guron lived here as a recluse, and after his death the Cornish St Petroc founded a priory in his memory in 550AD. Throughout the Middle Ages Bodmin was a favoured religious centre. The location of the Assize Courts here gave it the status of county town, which now properly belongs to Truro, seat of the county council. Whatever the rights of the matter, Bodmin with its substantial 19th-c. public buildings (Assize Courts, Shire Hall) has the air of an important town.

The priory, once the most important in the south-west, has disappeared. The town is now dominated by **St Petroc's Church**, the largest and one of the finest churches in the county. Built in the Perpendicular style (1467-71) on the site of an earlier Norman church, St Petroc's is recorded as costing a total of £268 11s 9½d, a sum to which the local guilds and townspeople were obliged to contribute. Those who were too poor to give money had to pay in kind or labour. The church boasts an outstanding Norman font carved with beasts and foliage, and Cornwall's finest effigy: the slate tomb of Prior Vyvyan (d. 1533) in the sanctuary. Also preserved in the church, in a glass case in the S wall, are the *Relics of St Petroc*. His bones were so holy and of such importance to the medieval monks that one stole them and took them to Brittany in 1170. They were only retrieved after threats of a punitive expedition from the king. In the churchyard E of the church are the ruins of the 14th-c. *Chantry Chapel of St Thomas à Becket*, and to the W *St Guron's Well*, the holy site which inspired St Petroc to found his priory here.

A less inspiring – but grimly historic – building is the *Old Prison* NW of the town, scene of public executions up to 1862. Many national treasures were stored here in World War 1, including the Domesday Book and the Crown Jewels.

On Beacon Hill above the town is the 144ft-high *obelisk* to Gen. Sir W.R. Gilbert (d. 1855), hero of the Sikh Wars, visible from many of the heights of Bodmin Moor. On the way out of Bodmin on the Lostwithiel Road is the *Regimental Museum of the Duke of Cornwall's Light Infantry*.

Two fine country houses near Bodmin are *Lanhydrock House* (NT) 2m S, and *Pencarrow House*, 3m N.

Bodmin Moor
E Cornwall

Bodmin Moor is a granite plateau of open heath, rough grass and heather, similar in character, geological age and formation to Dartmoor. However, it is smaller (only about 150 sq m), less famous and less wild than its sister in Devon. Also it is not a National Park but all privately owned, much of it by the Duchy of Cornwall. Nevertheless every Cornishman will swear that it is superior in beauty, views, antiquities and mystery.

The highest point on the moor is *Brown Willy* (from *bron ewhella*, Saxon for 'tallest hill') at 1375ft. The second highest is *Rough Tor* at 1311ft. Because the rest of the moor is relatively flat, these two tors rise above it like volcanic plugs and on clear days command views over much of Devon and Cornwall. Neither tor is particularly accessible by road. Brown Willy is best approached from Bolventor (4m) and Rough Tor from the end of the unclassified road off the A39 just N of Camelford (1½m).

The two tors are 2m apart. There are no footpaths to either and the walking is over rough moorland.

The granite of the moor, being very hard rock and submitting only to chemical weathering, forms tors – weird piles of boulders. The best known is *The Cheesewring*, near *St Cleer*. The erosion also causes very acid soil, which can only support moorland flora, such as heather and bracken, and in many places gives rise to peat bogs. Paradoxically, the very nature of the moor attracted prehistoric settlers: with their primitive tools they could not clear the thick woodland of the valleys, and on the moors there were no bears or other predators. Consequently the moor is thickly populated with important Bronze Age and Iron Age antiquities. Among the most interesting are the prehistoric hill-top fortresses of *Bury Castle* at *Cardinham* and *King Arthur's Hall* at *St Breward* and standing stones, circles and tombs in the parishes of *Blisland* and *St Cleer*.

The next people to inhabit the moor were the Celts, and the most famous of all Celts, King Arthur. Perhaps *Camelford* on the N edge of the moor was his Camelot, and *Slaughter Bridge* nearby, the site of his fatal last battle against his treacherous nephew Mordred. On his death, his sword Excalibur was returned to the mysterious *Dozmary Pool* at the very heart of the moor.

Subsequent inhabitants have been poor farmers living in isolated settlements on the moor by grazing sheep, or miners extracting granite for building and prospecting for tin and copper. The major mining area was around St Cleer, but old quarries and engine houses, the remains of extinct workings, are to be found all around the moor. Just off the moor near *St Neot*, the *Carnglaze Slate Caverns* are open to the public.

The centre of the moor has remained empty and unspoilt. There is almost nothing on the A30 except *Bolventor* with the famous *Jamaica Inn*, once an essential stopping place for all coaching (and smuggling!) traffic crossing the moor, and *Trewint Cottage* 5m further NE where John Wesley regularly stayed. Today, as in the past, the bulk of the population of the moor live in a ring of villages on the streams around the edge of the moor. Among them are some of the loveliest and least spoilt villages in Cornwall. For example *Altarnun*, *Blisland*, *Cardinham*, *St Neot*, *St Tudy* and *Warleggan*.

In the right weather conditions (watch for mist), Bodmin Moor offers excellent walking and motoring. (See *Walks 9 & 10*, p.24 and *Tour 6*, p.27.)

Bolventor 2C
Village on Bodmin Moor (A30), 10m NE of Bodmin

An isolated settlement in the middle of Bodmin Moor. There is little more than a tiny chapel of 1846 and the Georgian *Jamaica Inn*, made famous by Daphne du Maurier's novel of that name. The inn, which is slate-tile hung to protect it from the westerly winds of Bodmin Moor, originally served as a coaching house for traffic to Penzance, and was

also used for smuggling rum. At the end of the last century it suffered the indignity of becoming a temperance hostel, but now has a licence again and is deservedly popular with visitors.

The mysterious *Dozmary Pool* with its Arthurian associations is 2m S.

Boscastle 1C
Village on N coast (B3263), 3m NE of Tintagel

Boscastle Harbour (now National Trust) is the only harbour on this stretch of the coast and was therefore important from Norman times onwards despite the ferocious tidal surges and high cliffs, which caused numerous shipwrecks. It remained important until the coming of the railways in the 1890s.

The sea is not visible from the harbour, being at the end of the 'S'-shaped Cornish fjord: ships putting in had to negotiate some tricky rocks and were often assisted by other vessels or tow-ropes from the shore. From the village a path may be followed to the harbour, and over the rocks beyond it

Boscastle Harbour

for a view of the harbour entrance and sea. An hour before low tide an underwater fissure in the rocks causes dramatic spray effects from a 'blow-hole'.

To the W of the harbour, *Willapark Point* has fine cliff scenery, and the dramatic crater of the *Blackapit* slate quarry. Boat trips are available from the harbour (enquire at Pixie House) and there is a National Trust shop.

Bossiney 2C
Village on N coast (B3263). 3m SW of Boscastle

A tiny village near Tintagel with one of the few good bathing beaches on this rocky stretch of coast (*Bossiney Haven*). Overlooking the cove is the double headland of *Lye Rock*, with its colony of puffins, and *Willapark*, crowned by the ditch and rampart of an Iron Age fort. To the E of Bossiney is the wooded *Rocky Valley* with waterfalls and glens: a lovely spot.

Bossiney was once an important fishing community and in the Middle Ages had a castle. This disappeared in the 15th c., leaving only a *mound* (½m S). The mound is associated with King Arthur, claimed to be the site of his original Round Table. Every year, on Midsummer's Eve, the table is supposed to rise up and shine like silver.

Until the Great Reform Act of 1832 this tiny collection of farms and cottages was a 'rotten borough', electing two MPs. Of a total of 25 electors only nine – all from one family – ever exercised their franchise. Bossiney's most illustrious member was Sir Francis Drake.

Botallack 4C
Village on B3306, 8m NW of Penzance

One of the most romantic and famous of the ruined Cornish **tin mines**, with engine houses perched on cliffs above the sea. The engines pumped water out from the mines which had tunnels and galleries beneath the sea. The Atlantic could always be heard roaring above the miners' heads, and on a fateful day in 1893 it burst in, drowning 29 men 500ft down. Their bodies have never been recovered.

The mine, which operated from 1720-1914, once employed 500 people, making it one of the oldest and largest in Cornwall. Its construction was a great engineering feat, the working extending several hundred yards under the sea. Two of the engine houses are open to visitors: it is important to keep to the paths on the descent.

Breage 4A
Village on A394, 4m W of Helston

The richest tin mine in the county was in this parish. *Huel Vor* (Cornish for 'great work') had seams 30ft wide, worked at depths of up to 2500ft.

Today the greatest interest of the village lies in **St Breaca's Church**, supposedly founded by the Cornish saint in the Dark Ages but built in the 15th c., entirely of granite. Outside are grotesque heads and gargoyles on the tower, while inside on the N wall are delicate 15th-c. wall paintings, the most distinctive those of Christ of the Trades and of St Christopher carrying the boy Jesus. The murals were discovered when the church was being restored in 1891. The restorer, Edmund Sedding, made the rood screen in the medieval style. Also in the church is a Roman milestone (*c.* 268AD), the oldest in Cornwall and evidence that the Romans reached this part of the peninsula.

Bude 1C
Pop 5600. On N coast 27m SW of Bideford (A39). Events: Blessing of the sea (Aug), Carnival & Fete (3rd week Aug). EC Thur. Inf: Tel (0288) 4240

Originally part of the parish of Stratton, Bude developed as a seaport for the Bude Canal, built 1819-26, running 30m to Launceston. The canal was not, however, a commercial success and it was the fine beaches and airy situation which put Bude on the map as a popular family resort from Victorian times. Thanks to responsible ownership, much of the area is undeveloped, and Summerleaze Downs remains a refreshing open space. The long sandy beaches (*Summerleaze, Crooklets*) offer excellent bathing, and there are bathing pools providing alternative swimming at low tide (the tide goes out a long way).

The town's main street, the Strand, runs along the river to the S of the town, and from its foot the river is crossed for a visit to the *canal* (car park). Between the river and the canal is *The Castle*, a 19th-c. castellated folly built by Goldsworthy Gurney (1793-1875), inventor of the 'Bude Light' for lighthouses. The building is now used as council offices. The canal basin is the most attractive corner of the town, with its breakwater and lock at the seaward entrance (the canal is now only navigable for 1½m). On the wharf are two small museums: the *Bude Historical and Folk Exhibition* and the *Bude Militaria Museum*. On the far side of the canal to the S (on the road to Widemouth Bay) is *Ebbingford Manor* (15th-16th-c.).

Two neighbours of Bude with attractive churches can be seen in a short circuit from the town. 1m N is *Poughill*, ½m E is *Stratton*, the 'mother town' of Bude. 3m to the S, on the coast road, is *Widemouth Bay*, a splendid stretch of sandy beach (good surfing) in a ½m break in the rocky coastline.

Cadgwith   4A
Village on S coast off A3083, 4m NE of Lizard Point

A captivating village, unspoilt and very romantic, with the houses built of the local serpentine rock. ¼m S of the village is the **Devil's Frying Pan**, an enormous cavern whose roof fell in last century to leave a bowl, 200ft deep, which foams and spits at high tide. This wild coast – one of the most exciting stretches of the Cornwall Coast Path – is riddled with natural caves, but many of them can only be reached by boat. There is a circular cliff-top walk of 8m, starting in the village and going round *Lizard* Point to the beautiful *Kynance Cove*. (See *Walk 5*, p.25.) See also *Ruan Minor*.

Caerhays Castle   3B
Historic house off A3078, 12m S of St Austell

Although not open to the public, Caerhays is worthy of mention because of the impression on visitors who see it

from the road. In a marvellous position overlooking Veryan Bay, it is a castellated 'Gothick' castle of 1808 by John Nash (who also built Buckingham Palace and laid out Regents Park and its terraces in London). The extensive park, complete with landscaped lake and filled with rhododendrons, runs down to the road adjacent to the beach. The gardens are open to the public on two Sunday afternoons in April.

Callington   2D
Small town on A390, 10m S of Launceston Event: Honey Fair (Oct)

A small town of slate and granite houses over which rises the 1152ft *Kit Hill* topped with the tall chimney of a disused tin mine.

St Mary's Church was built in 1438 and has a prominent three-stage W tower and clerestory windows along the upper nave walls. (Clerestory windows are a rare feature in Cornish churches.) There are fine old wooden barrel roofs and a splendid, though damaged alabaster monument of 1502.

1m from the town centre is the **Dupath Well Chapel**, a 16th-c. chapel over an ancient holy well. For a long time the well was an important pilgrimage centre for the West Country, and the waters were believed to have curative properties. Today the water still flows through the squat granite building.

Calstock   2D
Village S of A390, 5m W of Tavistock

A river port on the banks of the Tamar in one of the least visited parts of Cornwall. The Tamar valley offers magnificent wooded scenery with superb views and good walks. The village is very pleasant if undistinguished, and has a heavily restored late 15th-c. church, *St Andrew's*, and an excellent waterside inn.

This was an important tin-mining area and there are numerous old engine houses in the valley around the village. The spectacular 12-arch *viaduct* carrying the old railway above the river is further evidence of the area's former industrial importance. The railway connected the

local mines with Calstock Quay until 1934, wagons being raised and lowered from the water by means of a lift.

Just W of the village is the beautiful medieval *Cotehele house, gardens and watermill (all National Trust).

Camborne   3A
Pop 16,631. 14m NE of Penzance (A30). EC Thur MD Fri

Camborne is famous for one thing – mining. It is the home of the internationally renowned Camborne School of Mines, founded in 1883 and the country's only school of metalliferous mining. Today its graduates get top jobs all over the world. Camborne was also the birthplace of Richard Trevithick (1771-1833) whose development of high-pressure steam pumps revolutionised mining. Until his work it had not been possible to pump water fast enough out of deep mines to enable men to go down them. With Watt and Stephenson he was also a pioneer of the locomotive, making and giving a trial run to the first high-pressure steam engine in Camborne. As a direct result of his invention Camborne's Dolcoath Mine became one of the deepest in the world, extracting ore from as far down as 3000ft.

Tin mining came to a virtual end in the 1930s after 160 years of feverish activity: the result of imports of cheap tin from Malaysia. However, one or two mines have recently started up again, and there are numerous plans to revive some of the richer seams.

There are many mementoes to the town's mining past. In front of the public library near the station is a *Statue of Trevithick*, and inside a *museum* of archaeology, mineralogy and local history. Just before *Pool* on the main road, at the **Camborne School of Mines**, there is an excellent *Museum of Geology*, displaying rocks and ores from around the world and showing the history of mining. 1/4m E, on either side of the road, are the **Cornish Engines** (NT). These two great beam engines, one a winding engine for taking men and ore up the shafts and the other

larger one for pumping water up to 2000ft, have been restored to working order.

Also associated with mining are Camborne's numerous chapels, Wesleyan halls and meeting houses: the miners' traditional places of worship and social gathering. With its unassuming two-storey buildings and general air of tranquillity Camborne is not an invigorating town and there is little relief in the sombre *Church of St Meriadocus*, a Victorian restoration of a 15th-c. building.

1m SE of the town at Lower Gryllis Farm, Treskillard, is the *Shire Horse and Carriage Museum*, a collection of horse-drawn vehicles and farming implements with pony and wagon rides a special attraction.

Almost contiguous with Camborne to the E is its sister mining town *Redruth and between the two to the S is the hill of *Carn Brea*.

Camelford   2C
Small town on A39, 16m W of Launceston

Is this King Arthur's Camelot? Many would like to think so and claim that **Slaughter Bridge** (1m N) is where the legendary king was mortally wounded in battle with his nephew Mordred in 542. Certainly the town is only a few miles from Tintagel, but the less romantically inclined suggest that the name is derived from a ford over the River Camel around which the town was built.

The town is an excellent centre for exploring the N coast and N Bodmin Moor; *Rough Tor*, the second highest point on the moor (1311ft) is only 4m SE and a passable road goes most of the way. There is a 6m circular walk climbing the tor (See *Walk 9*, p.25). Of greatest interest is the award-winning **North Cornwall Museum and Gallery** with fascinating exhibits recording local life (e.g. slate quarrying, shoe-making and carpentry) between 1890-1920. A special feature is the reconstruction of the upstairs and downstairs of an old moorland cottage.

Old engine house

The Parish **Church of St Julitta** is 1½m SW at *Lanteglos*, beautifully sited in a wooded valley by a stream. Although heavily restored, the church retains its original barrel roofs, the elegant 15th-c. granite arcade and some fragments of the 15th-c. glass. The tower is also 15th-c. In the churchyard is a 10th-c. Saxon pillar with runic inscriptions and four Celtic crosses.

2m S of the town is the lonely parish of *Advent* which has a fine parish *Church* with a Norman font and tall 14th-c. tower. 1m further S is *The Devil's Jump*, two granite outcrops, one 50ft high, facing each other across a ravine.

Cardinham
2C

Village on Bodmin Moor off A30, 4m E of Bodmin

Set in a moorland area densely covered with prehistoric barrows and hut circles, Cardinham is an interesting parish. The 15th-c. parish **Church of St Meubred** is typically Cornish, with its buttressed and pinnacled tower. In the churchyard is one of the finest *Celtic crosses* in the county – 8½ft high with knotwork and a 9th-c. inscription. Inside, the church has barrel roofs (the one in the nave a modern restoration) and finely carved 15th-c. bench ends. On the right of the altar is a historic brass of 1401 of an early incumbent, Thomas de Aumarle. On the wall of the N aisle are the plasterwork royal arms of Charles II (1661) and a panel recording a letter of thanks from Charles I to the inhabitants of Cornwall, given at the Royalist camp at Sudeley Castle, 1643. Unexpectedly, in such a remote part of Cornwall, the E window replaces one shattered by a bomb in 1942.

The scant remains of two fortifications lie within the parish. ¾m NE of the church is *Bury Castle*, a prehistoric earthwork; ½m S is *Cardinham Castle* mound, all that remains of the medieval Earls of Cornwall's castle.

Carn Brea
3A

Hill S of A30, between Camborne and Redruth

The road between Camborne and Redruth is dominated by this rocky height, topped by its obelisk. The approach for walkers is by footpaths from Carn Brea village to the N; for motorists by a lane from Carnkie to the S.

This hill has everything: outstanding views of much of Cornwall as well as the derelict mines of the area, a Stone Age hill fort and hut circles, a monument, the 90ft *Dunstanville Obelisk*, erected in 1837 to a local landowner, and a castle-style restaurant. It is the focus of legends of sleeping giants and treasure troves, many of which no doubt date from 1748 when Celtic gold coins were found here. Perhaps one day Carn Brea will be recalled for a modern ritual: the men with the nylon wings (known as 'hang-gliders') who launch themselves from the summit.

W of Carn Brea, on the Carnkie-Pool road, or reached directly from Pool (going S at the mini-roundabout to Four Lanes) is the *Carn Brea Leisure Centre*, W Cornwall's major sports and recreation complex. For a circular walk of 4½m starting in Carnkie and climbing Carn Brea, see Walk 8, p.25.

Carn Euny see *Sancreed*

Charlestown see *St Austell*

Cheesewring see *St Cleer*

Chun Castle see *Madron*

Chysauster
4C

Ancient site off B3311, 4m N of Penzance

Maintained by the Department of the Environment, this is the largest and best preserved Iron Age village site in Cornwall, and well worth a visit (approached by minor road off B3311 at Badger's Cross). A footpath leads uphill from the car park to a village 'street' of eight dwellings, probably built *c.* 100BC and occupied into the Roman period. The survival of dwellings of this period in a street is very rare, as they were usually made of mud and wood and have long since disappeared. These were substantial houses of stone with walls up to 15ft thick, paved floors and thatched roofs. Built around court-yards, the dwellings were occupied by farmers and tin-streamers and the archeological evidence suggests that the tin may have been exported as far as France and the Mediterranean. Other courtyard houses have also been found in the area.

The lack of any fortification at Chysauster can be related to its location near the Iron Age hill fort of *Castle-an-Dinas* on the summit 1m E. The latter, crowned by an 18th-c. folly (*Roger's Tower*) is the highest point in W Cornwall (765ft). The fort once had massive concentric rings, but much of the stone has been removed over the centuries, some of it to build the folly.

A lay-by on the road below Castle-an-Dinas offers a splendid view of Penzance and the S coastline of the peninsula.

Constantine   4A
Village off B3291, 6m SW of Falmouth

A large hill-top village at the head of the River Helford, set in beautiful varied countryside. The large *Church*, to the saint after whom the village is named, is mainly 15th-c., and has an impressive W tower. *The Queen's Arms* is an excellent old inn.

¹/₂m N of the village on the B3291 is the lovely Georgian *Trewardreva Manor House* (not open) and opposite, the *Pixie's Hall* and underground curved passage or fogou, 66ft long, 6ft high and originally within a walled enclosure. Its purpose – ritual, defensive or for storage – for Prehistoric man is not known, but it is now occupied by spritely pixies.

Cornwall Coast Path see *Walks*, p.24

Cotehele (NT)   2D
Historic house off A390, 7m E of Callington

Described as the finest late-medieval manor in the country, Cotehele came to the Edgcumbe family in 1353 and remained theirs until they gave it to the National Trust in 1947. The original manor of 1353 was largely rebuilt 1485-1539, and apart from the addition of the tower in 1627 and restoration of the private chapel in the last century, the house has not changed since. It consists of an entrance gateway, two courtyards, a chapel, great hall and numerous rooms all filled with the family's original 16th-18th-c. furniture, four-poster beds, tapestries, armour and weaponry. Charles II stayed here and George III, Queen Victoria and Prince Albert all visited to see the house in its romantic wooded position above the River Tamar. The gardens, sloping down to the E, are terraced with ponds and waterfalls. There is also a medieval dovecote and the (restored and working) manorial *watermill* and *cider-press* by the river.

At *Cotehele Quay* ¹/₂m S are 18th-c. and Victorian warehouses, the *National Maritime Museum Gallery* and *Shamrock*, a Tamar sailing barge (all **NT**).

Coverack   4A
Village on S coast (B3294), 10m SE of Helston

A beautiful unspoilt Cornish fishing village on a wild and exciting stretch of the coast. The bay, away from any major settlement and in a remote part of the county, was once a notorious smuggling centre. Inland is the flat moorland of Goonhilly Downs (see *★St Keverne*).

Crackington Haven   1C
Inlet on N coast off A39, 6m NE of Boscastle

Situated in the centre of a 5m stretch of cliff owned by the National Trust, Crackington Haven had the reputation of a graveyard for the sailing ships which tried – and often failed – to put in here. The rocky beach has sand at low tide and there are superb cliff walks on the Cornwall Coast Path, N to *Millook Haven* and S to *★Boscastle*.

Crantock   3A
Village off A3075, 3m SW of Newquay

A pleasant village on the S bank of the Gannel estuary opposite Newquay. Until the Gannel silted up this was a busy port – long before the development of Newquay. It was also an important religious centre, stemming from the time that the legendary Celtic missionary St Carantoc arrived here in the 5th c.

Overleaf: Cadgwith

The Norman **St Carantoc's Church**, rebuilt in the 15th c. after the tower had collapsed through the nave, was further reconstructed in 1902. The present building is worth visiting for its interior, sensitively treated in the spirit of the original. The screen is exceptionally fine and the chancel retains some of the old Norman masonry. In the churchyard are the old village stocks with a memorial to the last person held in them, William Tinney.

There is a lovely walk W along the Gannel estuary past Crantock Beach to *Pentire West Point* (2m). For other walks in the area, see *★Newquay*.

Cubert 3A
Village off A3075, 4m SW of Newquay

For those making a detour to Holywell Bay, this village is worth a pause for its attractive **Church of St Cubertus** with its 14th-c. tower and spire. (Spires are unusual in Cornwall, particularly the broached spire seen here.) The church has a Norman granite font and a pulpit made up of old bench ends. The church was restored in 1852 by G.E. Street.

The sandy beach at *Holywell Bay* is National Trust property, as is Cubert Common behind: this has saved the area from development. Swimming here is dangerous, so it is best just to enjoy the view of the dramatic rock formations and perhaps at low tide to climb the 15 steps on the N side of the bay to the cave where lies the *Holy Well of St Cubertus*.

Delabole 2C
Village on B3314, 3m W of Camelford

Delabole, a miners' village, is famous for the **slate quarry**, the largest man-made hole in England, 400ft deep and 1½m in circumference. It may have been worked by the Romans and has been worked continuously since Elizabethan times. The quarry is not open, but there is a viewing platform from which visitors can look into the vast void. The slate is used all over the country for roofing, building and church headstones, but the quarry's livelihood is increasingly threatened by plastic slates.

Devoran 3A/4A
Village on A39, 5m S of Truro

Once a busy port exporting tin and copper, Devoran was largely built (1820-39) to house tin-streamers and miners. Though it perfectly retains its character there are now few traces of its former industry. The *Church* was built in the 1880s by J.L. Pearson, later the architect of Truro Cathedral.

Dobwalls 2C
Village on A38, 3m W of Liskeard

The *Forest Railroad Park* is a Mecca for all railway enthusiasts, with American railroads in miniature. There is a 1m track of model passenger steam railway based on a stretch of the Denver and Rio Grande railroad, and another based on the Union Pacific. Also loco sheds, a picnic area, cafe and 'hall of memories'. The *Thorburn Museum and Art Gallery* has a fine collection of wildlife pictures by *Archibald Thorburn* (1860-1935).

Dozmary Pool 2C
Natural feature on Bodmin Moor, 1½m S of A30 at Bolventor

This is the melancholy site of two legends. Here the mortally wounded King Arthur came to return his mystical sword Excalibur before dying. As he threw the sword to the centre of the lake a hand rose up, taking the sword and

slowly drawing it under the water. The second legend concerns the evil steward Tregeagle, who, for his exploitation and treachery, was condemned to the task of emptying the limitless pool with a limpet shell. Whenever the wind blows he can be heard howling. Sadly, the story that the pool is bottomless was disproved 100 years ago when it dried up. The historic *Jamaica Inn* is 1½m N at *Bolventor*.

Ship's figurehead, Falmouth

Falmouth 4A

Pop 17,530. 9m S of Truro (A39). Events: Spring Flower (late Mar), Regatta week (mid Aug). EC Wed. Inf: Tel (0326) 312300

Beautifully situated on the Fal Bay (known as Carrick Roads), Falmouth is one of the most delightful towns in Cornwall. First and foremost is a superb natural harbour. There is evidence that it was used by the Phoenicians in search of tin and then by the Romans. But there was no town at all in the Middle Ages. When Sir Walter Raleigh put in here on returning from Guinea he found only Arwenack, the seat of the Killigrew family and one other house. However, Raleigh recognised the potential of the harbour and persuaded the Killigrews to develop the town – despite strenuous opposition from the ports of Truro and Penryn.

Falmouth grew quickly; the Customs House moved from Penryn in 1652 and in 1660 the town was given its name (previously it had been known as Pen-y-cwm-wick or Penny-come-quick). A few years later a writer noted that it was a 'haven very notable and famous, and in a manner the most principal in all Britayne'. It was the headquarters of the Mail Packet trade until it lost it to Southampton in 1852, which precipitated a slump only alleviated when the railway arrived in 1863 bringing visitors, new hotels, smart houses and trade. It has remained an important port and can take ships of up to 90,000 tons in the dry docks (opened in 1958 by the Queen). The USSR factory fishing fleet regularly uses Falmouth as a repair port. Today it is popular with yachtsmen.

Overleaf: Fowey

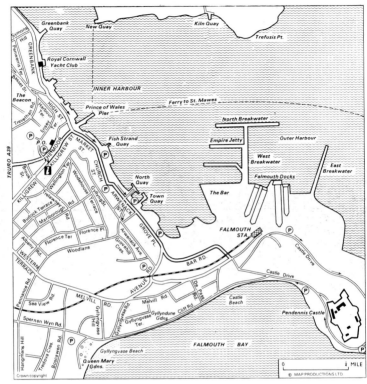

Falmouth

Through routes   → One-way streets   Ⓟ Parking

Pendennis Castle, Falmouth

The old part of the town consists of one long road running from Penryn towards Pendennis Point, with the buildings getting progressively older towards the harbour. On either side are *opes*, narrow covered passages or openings leading down to the harbour or connecting streets higher up the hill. Many of the opes near the harbour have interesting shops and bistros.

The **Church of King Charles the Martyr**, built in 1665, is dedicated to the monarch in recognition of the town's loyalty to the Royalist cause in the Civil War. Charles II personally sponsored the building. It is not especially attractive, but is unusual for its narrow rectangular tower. On the other side of the road is the beautiful Doric-style *Customs House* of 1820. It was a great boost to the town – at the expense of Penryn – when it was built here. Behind it is the *King's Pipe*, a brick chimney in which the excise men burnt contraband tobacco. It still occasionally has a smoke!

Moored in the Customs House quay is the *St Denys*, an old Falmouth pilot vessel. Open to the public, who can see the captain's quarters and men's rooms, it forms the nucleus of the *Falmouth Maritime Museum*. The rest of the collection (models, maps etc) lacks a home at present, but one is being actively sought.

Further S is a squat obelisk to the Killigrew family (1737), the town's founders, and on the other side of the road *Arwenack House*, their Tudor mansion, currently being restored and converted into flats. 2m further S, reached by the beautiful *Castle Drive*, is **Pendennis Castle**. Henry VIII built a 2-storey circular keep before the town was in existence to protect the harbour from the French. Elizabeth I reinforced it with defensive ramparts. It played an important part in the Civil War; Charles I's wife (and later his son Prince Charles) stayed here for protection before fleeing the country. The castle was subsequently heroically defended by the 70-year-old Sir John Arundell for 6 months before the starving troops had

to surrender – surviving longer than any other castle under siege in the country. The castle commands superb views inland over the town, S towards the Lizard and W, beyond St Anthony's Head towards Torpoint.

In S Falmouth there are bathing beaches but only *Gyllyngvase Beach* is sandy at all tides. There are ferries from the harbour to *St Mawes and *Flushing and, in summer, excursions around the harbour and up the river to *Truro. *Glendurgan Gardens (NT) are 5m SW.

Flushing   4A
Village 2m E of Penryn, ½m from Falmouth by ferry

Founded by Dutch immigrants in the 17th c., Flushing is reputed to have the warmest climate in Cornwall. It still has a Dutch air, with tall 18th-c. houses on the waterfront. The best are slate-hung. When the steam packets ran from Falmouth, the village was an important centre, benefiting from the trade; now it is much quieter but still very attractive with beautiful views across the Carrick Roads (the name of the bay). See also *Falmouth and *Mylor Bridge.

Fowey   3C
Town on A3082, 9m E of St Austell. Event: Royal Regatta & Carnival (2nd or 3rd week of Aug) EC Wed. Inf: Tel (072683) 3320

One of Cornwall's most picturesque towns, consisting of long narrow streets with numerous steps and alleys leading off down to the estuary or up the steep hill. It is a superb natural harbour, safe in storms and easily defended; its great historical importance is entirely due to this fact.

In the Middle Ages Fowey was one of the country's most important ports, supplying men and vessels for every battle against the Scots or French. In 1347, 47 ships (a number second only to Yarmouth) sailed from Fowey to attack Calais. Crusaders sailed from Fowey to the Holy Land, and tin was traded for Bordeaux wine. But in addition to these legitimate activities 'Fowey Gallants' (or pirates as their enemies might have called them) raided and plundered foreign shipping and Continental ports.

(part 14th-c., part 1782) and two admirable historic pubs. *The Ship Inn* dates back to Elizabeth I and was formerly a town house, and *The King of Prussia*, overlooking the quay on granite pillars, is a far grander building than the town hall. It was once run by the notorious smuggler, John Carter (self-styled 'King of Prussia') who presumably used it as an outlet for his contraband liquor. The *Noah's Ark Folk Museum* is in Fore Street.

There are two ferries from Fowey. A passenger ferry crosses to **Polruan**, a delightful village on the opposite promontory. Polruan has a strongly Mediterranean character, with narrow alleys of steep steps leading to colour-washed cottages. Quite apart from its own charms it should be visited for its views back across the estuary to Fowey. The other ferry (which takes vehicles) crosses to *Bodinnick*, also a delightful village, but much smaller. There is a really good round walk using both ferries from Fowey to the two villages (see *Walk 6*, p.25). See also *Golant.

Germoe 4D
Village on A394, 5m W of Helston

St Germoe's Church is supposed to have been founded by the Irish saint king on a visit to Cornwall in 460 AD, but the building is mostly 15th-c. with some Norman work. In the NE corner of the churchyard is *St Germoe's Chair*, a medieval structure of pointed arches and granite columns with triple seats inside. It is unique and its purpose is a mystery.

1m S, between the village and Praa Sands, is the late medieval *Pengersick Castle* (not open) with battlements and towers.

Glendurgan Gardens (NT) 4A
Nr Mawnan Smith, 6m SW of Falmouth

Beautiful gardens set in steep valleys with flowering shrubs, mature trees, a water garden and walled garden, the Giant's Steps and a maze.

Godolphin House 4D
Historic house off B3302, 5m NW of Helston

Set in romantic surroundings marked by the ruins of old tin workings (which once belonged to the owners), Godolphin House is the former home of the (now extinct) Earls of Godolphin. The 1st Earl was Queen Anne's Lord Chancellor – the most powerful man in the country – at the beginning of the 18th c. The house is built around three sides of a square with an impressive loggia of massive Tuscan granite columns on the N front. Basically early Tudor, it was enlarged in Elizabethan times, and again under Charles I and Queen Anne, and some of the rooms still have early linenfold panelling, elaborate plaster ceilings and carved fireplaces.

Golant 3C
Village off B3269, 3m N of Fowey

A charming village on the steep shore of the River Fowey with a little quay, excellent inn, *The Fisherman's Arms*, and a small but interesting church. *St Sampson* was built in 1509 and has a fine barrel roof and carved bench ends. By the S porch is a holy well whose waters were once thought to have healing properties. 1m W on the B3269 is **Castle Dore**, a prehistoric earthwork which is reputed to have been the site of the castle of King Mark of Cornwall. He

entertained Arthur and the Knights of the Round Table here and his nephew, Tristram is said to be buried here. It was Tristram and his wife Isolde who inspired Wagner's operatic *Ring Cycle*. Centuries later, in 1644, Charles I slept on the site in his coach before defeating the Parliamentarians in one of the last Royalist victories of the Civil War.

Goonhilly Downs see *St Keverne*

Gweek   4A
Village on B3291, 4m E of Helston

An attractive little village on the tidal reaches of the River Helford. In the 14th c. it was an important port, but is now notable for the **Cornish Seal Sanctuary**. Set up in 1958, there are five pools where seals, porpoises, dolphins and sea birds are tended before being returned to the wild. Seals breed around the Cornish coast in the winter months and victims of pollution, oil and gales are brought here in an attempt to conserve the endangered species. There are no baby seals at the sanctuary over the summer. There is a good pub, and excellent cream teas are to be had in the village.

3m SE is *Trelowarren* historic house.

Gwennap   3A
Village off A393, 3m SE of Redruth. Event: Annual Methodist Gathering (Spring Bank Hol Mon)

It has been claimed that more copper and tin has been extracted from this parish than any other in Europe. It is filled with the relics of disused mine workings: shafts, engine houses, spoil heaps and old engine tracks, although the village itself is delightfully placed in oak and beech woods away from the mines.

1m E of Redruth is **Gwennap Pit**, an amphitheatre caused by mining subsidence. Landscaped in 1803, the pit has perfect acoustics and was where John Wesley, the founder of Methodism, preached on a number of occasions to up to 20,000 people. He last preached here in 1789, and his visits are now commemorated with annual Methodist gatherings on Whitsun Monday.

Gwithian   4D
Village on N coast (B3301), 5m NW of Camborne

There is a sharp change in the scenery of the N coast at Gwithian. To the N are rocky slate cliffs with exciting cliff-top walks to *Godrevy Point* (2m). Beyond is Godrevy Island with an unmanned lighthouse of 1859. The coast path continues round the headland past Navax Point to *Hell's Mouth* (4m), an alarmingly sheer cliff of 100ft where the B3301 meets the coast.

To the W of the village are *towans* – rolling sand-dunes. Beneath the sands are buried houses and a very early chapel which was briefly uncovered last century revealing human skeletons, before being swept back under the sands during a gale. Its location is now lost.

Harlyn Bay   2B
On N coast off B3276, 3m W of Padstow

A sheltered sandy beach with a stream and rock pools. Most interesting is the site of an *Iron Age cemetery*, discovered under the sand dunes in 1900. About 150 slate coffins with remains buried about 2000 years ago were unearthed here.

1m NW, at *Trevose*, a short toll road can be taken to *Trevose Head*, a projecting headland which has a long history of shipwrecks. There is a lighthouse on the head and a lifeboat station (Padstow's) in Mother Ivey's Bay.

Hayle   4D
Town on N coast (A30), 7m NE of Penzance

In 1859 a traveller wrote that the town 'consists chiefly of mean cottages, a few poor shops, an inn, and a shabby railway viaduct'. Most visitors do not take so violently against Hayle, but it is widely regarded as somewhere to drive through on the way to Land's End. However, the town has some attractive Regency cottages, a once commercial harbour and the industrial archeological relics of the important foundries that once made castings of mining equipment used in every Cornish mine and exported all over the world.

Just W of the town centre off the B3302 is *Bird Paradise*, where there are more than 300 birds including penguins, flamingoes, toucans and owls in 7 acres of gardens. In addition there is a small farm and the *Paradise Brewery* where visitors can see 'real ale' brewed.

At The Towans (1m N of the town centre) a passenger-carrying *Miniature Railway* is laid out in the dunes, with a 40ft tunnel and other interesting features. 2m E of Hayle (turn off A30 for Gwinear) past the level crossing is the *Gwinear Outdoor Model Railway*. An '00' gauge railway follows 3000ft of splendidly landscaped track.

Helston   4A
Pop 10,570. 13m E of Penzance (A394). Events: Furry Day (May 8), Harvest Fair (1st week Sep) EC Wed MD Sat.

A really lovely old town, founded by the Saxons, with a charter from King John, and granted the right of making tin coins under Edward I.

Helston is most famous for its annual festival – *Furry Day* or Flora Day, which is almost certainly pre-Christian in origin. On May 8 every year, everyone in the town stops working and, to the sound of ringing bells, spends the day dancing through decorated streets. At midday the town's dignitaries join the dancing in the formal regalia of mayoral chains, top hats and tails. The ancient holiday is said to be older than the town. One day a minor devil – feeling restless – decided to bring one of the huge granite rocks from the gates of hell with him on a trip to Cornwall. But he was stopped by St Michael (so the post-pagan version of the story goes) and dropped the Hell-Stone (Helston) here and fled back to the underworld. So the locals have always celebrated his departure, and until this century people who failed to join the merrymaking were thrown in the river.

Church Street is a beautifully curved street of Georgian houses with a Georgian church of 1765 at one end and the Market Hall of 1838 at the other. *Coinagehall Street* and *Meneage Street* are both excellent Georgian shopping streets, the former unusually broad with a 20th-c. Gothic gateway at the end. The town *Museum* (behind the Town Hall) has a good collection of agricultural implements and items of local history.

The *Aero Park and Flambards Village* on the SE side of the town is a large leisure park with a collection of historic aircraft, vintage Ford cars, Battle of Britain memorabilia and a simulated Concorde flight deck. The Flambards village of cobbled streets, carriages, shops and all the period trimmings is based on the well-known television series.

The seal sanctuary at *Gweek* is 4m E, the beautiful harbour at *Porthleven* 2m SE and the Poldark Mine at *Wendron*, 3m NE. The *Penrose Walks* (NT) along *The Loe*, Cornwall's largest lake, are deservedly famous. The walks along the water through cedar woods lead to *The Loe* and *Porthleven Sands* (3m). A circular walk of 7m, through the Penrose Walks and along the coast path is described. (See Walk 4, p.24.)

Kilkhampton 1C
Village on A39, 6m NE of Bude

A hill-top village in the most N part of Cornwall. The village has always been associated with the Grenville family, who were granted the manor by William the Conqueror, and still retain the right to appoint the parish vicar. Their medieval castle (½m W of the village) is now nothing but a mound and their mansion at Stowe (3m W), once the finest house in the county, was dismantled in 1739.

St James's Church in the village is a late 15th-c. building which retains a Norman S door from the original church. The door has the classic Norman decorations of zig-zag and dog-tooth patterns. Inside are 157 beautifully carved bench ends (16th-c.) and the Grenville Chapel, with a monument to the Royalist hero Sir Bevil Grenville who fought at Stamford Hill. Note also the royal arms of Charles II.

The lovely **Coombe Valley**, much of it owned by the NT, runs from just N of

the village 4m to the sea at Duckpool Bay. There is an interesting 1½m *Nature Trail* through mixed woodland in the valley bottom, starting 3m W at Coombe. (See also *Walk 1*, p.24.)

Kingsand and Cawsand 3D
Villages on S coast off B3247, 5m SW of Plymouth via Torpoint car ferry

Delightful twin villages with steep streets and marvellous views over Plymouth Sound – always filled with ships and yachts – towards the Plymouth Breakwater. Until the breakwater was created last century from millions of tons of rubble, the approach to the Devonport Docks was impossible in rough seas and ships had to shelter in Cawsand Bay.

2m N of the village is *Mount Edgcumbe* park and historic house. It can be reached by road or along an interesting stretch of the Cornwall coastal path (3m). The path leads S to Penlee Point (2m) and *Rame Head* where there is a tiny semi-ruined chapel of 1397. (See also *Walk 7*, p.25).

9m SW of Rame Head is the Eddystone Lighthouse. The present lighthouse is the fourth on the dangerous rocks. The first, built in 1697, was the first in the world to be built out to sea, and lasted only five years before burning down. The second was washed away and the third, now called Smeaton's Tower, stands on Plymouth Hoe.

Kynance Cove 4A
2m N of Lizard Point

One of the wonders of the Cornish coast, the cove was described in a Victorian guidebook as 'wild and shaggy, where, in the scene that opens before him, the traveller may find realised some of the glowing fancies of fairyland'. The attraction of the cove lies in the white sand (only uncovered for 2½ hrs each side of low tide) and the dark green polished serpentine rock which is moulded into caverns like *The Kitchen* and *The Parlour* or spectacular rocks like *Gull Rock* and *Asparagus Island*. *The Devil's Letterbox* and *The Bellows* are blowing holes through

which the ocean is propelled with great force and a ferocious roaring noise.

Fortunately this outstanding stretch of coast is preserved by the National Trust and is all worth exploring. The walk to the cove from *Lizard Point* is only 2m and extremely rewarding. A fine cliff-top walk of 8m starts at *Cadgwith*, leaving the coast at Kynance Cove. (See *Walk 5*, p.25.)

Lamorna 4C
Village on S coast off B3315. 5m SW of Penzance

A pretty village that runs along the lane down through the wooded gorge-like valley to Lamorna Cove. Half way down the valley, by the river, the *Old Mill* has been converted to a craft centre. Further down the valley is the excellent, though oddly-named *Lamorna Wink Inn*. Although the cove itself is rocky, the harbour – protected by a jetty – is sandy. Most summers there is an exhibition of the work of local artists in a house above the harbour.

W of the Lamorna Road, on the B3315, are three very accessible and interesting prehistoric monuments. The first, about ½m from the Lamorna turning on the N (right side of the road) is the *Two Pipers*, two upright stones, both more than 13ft high, 120ft apart in two adjacent fields. Beyond them, on the other side of the road are the **Merry Maidens**, a complete circle of 19 standing stones, 78ft in diameter. Although the circle has been accurately dated to 2400BC, there is a local story that these stones are the earthly remains of some girls who broke the Sabbath by dancing. The *Two Pipers* who were playing for them were also punished by being turned to stone. 200yds on, on the same side, is the Bronze Age *Tregiffian Barrow*, a chamber tomb at the roadside, which when excavated revealed bones, charcoal and an undamaged funerary urn.

Land's End 4C
10m W of Penzance (A30)

The most westerly point in England, beyond which lies the vast Atlantic. Thus, as a Victorian traveller observed

profoundly, 'the view from so commanding point necessarily includes a wide expanse of ocean.' However there is a little more than sea. 1½m out is the *Longships Lighthouse* with a helicopter platform on top. 8m further out is the *Wolf Rock Lighthouse* and 28m SW, only visible on a clear day, are the Isles of Scilly, especially beautiful at sunset.

The English Channel meets the Atlantic at Land's End and the confluence of the oceans causes very rough waters. 60ft waves are not unusual in a storm – higher than the Longships lighthouse.

The whole site has recently been sold, and there are ambitious plans for removing some of the unsightly huts that spoil the area around the headland. *The Land's End* pub will remain and conservation work will be done to prevent erosion. But even the car parks and gift shops cannot detract from the grandeur of the ocean stretching for 3000 miles to the Americas.

There is an 8m circular walk from the car park at Land's End, taking in some of the dramatic coastline. (See *Walk 3*, p.24.) See also *Sennen*.

Lanhydrock House (NT) 3C
Historic house off B3268, 3m SE of Bodmin

Considered Cornwall's finest country house, Lanhydrock is beautifully set in 750 acres of park and woodland, in the parish of the same name.

The manor of Lanhydrock was purchased by Richard Robartes, a Truro merchant, in 1620: by 1651 the house which he started was completed by his son John, the second Lord Robartes. The house, built of grey granite, originally comprised four wings enclosing a courtyard, but in 1789 the E wing was removed, leaving three sides of a square. In 1881 a fire destroyed the whole house, with the exception of the N wing, porch and gatehouse. It was immediately rebuilt, using the same local granite (the later wings are indistinguishable from the old parts), but the interior decor and furnishings were Victorian.

Of the original 17th-c. house there are some interesting survivals. The *Gatehouse*, approached by a splendid avenue running down to the River Fowey, is a charming and fanciful two-storey building topped by obelisks. The porch of the main house retains its coat of arms and the *Gallery* (116ft long) in the N wing its splendid plaster ceiling (1640) illustrating scenes from the Old Testament. The kitchen and servants' quarters (now used as a restaurant) have their original fixtures and equipment.

The formal gardens to the N and E of the house were laid out by Sir George G. Scott in 1857. Above the house stands the 15th-c. parish *Church of St Hydrock*, restored at the same time as the house. The surrounding parkland is ideal for walks.

Lappa Valley Railway see *Newquay*

Launcells   1C
Village off A3072, 4m E of Bude

In a secluded valley is the 15th-c. **St Andrew's Church**, one of the best preserved in Cornwall and unspoiled by over-zealous restoration. The church retains attractive barrel roofs over the N and S aisles and superbly-carved bench ends and box pews in the N aisle. There are fragmentary wall paintings and the chancel has a variety of tiles made in Barnstaple in the 15th c. Opposite the S end of the church, by the stream, is *St Swithin's Holy Well*.

Launceston   2D
Town on A30, 22m NE of Bodmin. Event:
Agricultural Show (Jun). EC Thur; MD Tue & Sat

Lauscavetone of the Domesday Book, Launceston is the 'Gateway to Cornwall', the first town that most visitors reach on their way west. It has had a mayor since 1257 and was the county town until it lost the privilege to Bodmin in 1835. Today it has the feel of an important centre, even though its population is not much more than 5000.

St Mary Magdalene, described as the finest church W of Exeter, can certainly claim the best carving in the West Country. The tower is late 14th-

c., but the body of the church dates from 1511-24. The exterior is covered, all over, in panels of foliage, shields, saints and prayers (including the Ave Maria). No space is left uncarved, and all the work is in granite, notorious for its hardness and resistance to cutting. The entire church was paid for by Sir Henry Trecarel. He had intended the panels for his manor house, but when his wife and only son both died he abandoned work on his home and threw all his efforts into this remarkable building. Inside are some good monuments, the royal arms of King George I, and a rare painted pulpit at least 450 years old.

From St Mary's, Church Street leads towards *Southgate Arch*: all that remains of the old town walls which once surrounded the city. Launceston, as the seat of the Earls of Cornwall, was the only strongly fortified city in the county. The arch houses an interesting craft gallery.

The town's central *Market Square* (between Broad Street and High Street) is an attractive assemblage of 17th-18th c. shops and houses including *The White Hart Hotel*, an excellent old coaching inn for travellers to Penzance. The 12th-c. doorway incongruously placed in the classical façade is the chief remnant of Launceston's once powerful priory. From the market it is a short walk to the **Castle**. Of Celtic origins, the castle was rebuilt by Edward the Confessor, again by King William and enlarged by the Black Prince. It was the stronghold of the powerful Earls of Cornwall until the Earldom (later a Duchy) passed to the Crown. Today the castle belongs to Prince Charles as Duke of Cornwall. It consists of a gatehouse and central circular double-walled keep on a motte. The views from the top are marvellous, of Bodmin Moor to the W, Dartmoor to the E and the Tamar Valley to the N and S.

Just N of the castle and no less sturdily built is the *Doomsdale Prison*, a ruined single cell in which George Fox, the founder of Quakerism, was imprisoned in unspeakable conditions

for his opinions in 1656. Until 1821, the area outside the prison was used for public hangings. The arch which is part of the prison building leads into the delightful Georgian *Castle Street*, with red-brick and tile-hung houses of substance. Two of the best are open to the public, one as *The Eagle Hotel* and the other as **Lawrence House Museum** (NT). Still used as the mayor's parlour, it serves as the borough museum and is full of extraordinary objects such as Victorian patent vacuum cleaners and washing machines.

¼m N, at the bottom of a very steep hill that was part of the town's natural defences, is the delightful little River Kensey. The road crosses it on an 18th-c. bridge, but just upstream is the medieval *Priory Footbridge*, only 4ft wide. Behind it is *St Thomas's Church*, built near the site of the old priory and a parish church since 1539, with a fine Norman font.

Lelant   4D
Small town on A3074, 8m NE of Penzance, 3m SE of St Ives

Until the Hayle estuary silted up, this small town was a busy port. It is now a quiet residential place, with the St Ives golf course and the beaches of St Ives Bay near to hand. The **Church of St Uny** stands on the site of a building put up by an Irish missionary of that name in the 6th c. Parts of the Norman church which replaced it survive in this later, 15th-c. building – namely the font and part of the arcade to the N aisle. In the town is the *Lelant Model Village*, with its models of well-known Cornish buildings and *museum* of Cornish history.

2m W of Lelant is *Trencrom*, an Iron Age fort on a hill-top preserved by the National Trust.

Liskeard   2C/2D
Town on A38, 15m NW of Plymouth. Events: Carnival Week (late Jun), Fat Stock Show (mid-Nov). EC Wed MD Mon (cattle and sheep) & Thur

A lively market town and the centre of a fertile agricultural area, Liskeard was once an important stannary town surrounded by prosperous copper

mines. The mines are all gone. The town is built across a steep valley and has many unexpectedly exciting views and vistas. It has no buildings of outstanding merit but is full of pleasant Georgian and Victorian cottages and houses. The grandest building in town is *Webb's Hotel* (1828) in the Old Market Place. The town is of greatest interest to the visitor as a first-rate shopping centre.

2m W at *Dobwalls* is the Forest Railroad Park and 3m S at *St Keyne*, the Paul Corin Collection of old musical instruments.

Lizard   4A
Headland on S coast (A3083), 11m S of Helston

The most southerly point in Britain, a heather-covered headland with outstanding cliff scenery, ranking amongst the finest in the country.

Lizard Village is a somewhat ramshackle place with huts where craftsmen carve objects from serpentine, the rare semi-precious rock found only on this peninsula. The village merges at its E end with the much prettier *Landewednack*, full of colour-washed cottages set amidst trees. **The Church of St Winwallo** – the southernmost in England – is built from the local dark green serpentine. It is 15th-c., retaining a Norman porch.

This treacherous coast, which has had more than its share of shipwrecks, is protected by a lighthouse at **Lizard Point** built in 1756 on the site of a wooden one of 1619. Of necessity it has one of the most powerful lights in the country, and is visible 22m out to sea. It is open to the public on weekday afternoons (1-5) when there is no fog. In either direction lies spectacular cliff scenery. To the W is *Polpeor Cove*, riddled with caverns and caves; to the E is *Lion's Den*, a large funnel with the sea swirling at the bottom, created when a cavern collapsed last century. See also *Cadgwith*, *Ruan Minor* and *Kynance Cove*, all of which can be reached by foot along the coastal path or by car. There is a walk along the coast path from Cadgwith to Kynance Cove. (See *Walk 5*, p.25.)

Looe
3C

Town on S coast (A387), 8m S of Liskeard. Event: International Sea Angling Festival (Sep). EC Thur. Inf: Tel (05036) 2072

Divided into East and West by its river, the two halves of Looe are dramatically sited on steep wooded hills on either side of the estuary. The narrow streets of whitewashed stone cottages are a perfect complement to their magical setting. (Note: Looe gets extremely crowded in the summer and cars should be parked in East Looe by the bridge, from where the town can easily be explored by foot.)

Looe was a great port in the Middle Ages and Tudor times, supplying ships for every important sea battle including the Siege of Calais (1346) and The Armada (1588). It was also an important fishing port, and there are still a few **working boats to be seen** in the harbour, attracting hundreds of noisy seagulls. Visitors can go out on deep-sea fishing expeditions and in addition to mackerel, herring and bass, sharks – some weighing up to 100lbs – are regularly landed. (Sharks are caught 10-20m offshore, and are no threat to bathers.) The International Sea Angling Festival is held here each September, when all facilities are laid on for the expert competitive angler.

East Looe is the larger part of the town. From the bridge, Fore Street runs S past the new Guildhall to the old quarter and the quay. In High Market Street is the *Old Guildhall* (16th-c.) which once contained the law courts and now has a *museum* with objects of local interest, many relating to an important regional 'industry' – smuggling. This is ironic, because smuggling cases were never heard in the town law courts: the prosecutors would have been unable to get a conviction. To the S is the *quay*, with its old warehouses and boat sheds and small *aquarium*, and a fine sandy beach protected by a jetty (Banjo Pier).

West Looe has the interesting *Church of St Nicholas*, founded c. 1330. The tower once contained a 'scold's cage' for nagging women. *The Jolly Sailor Inn* is 16th-c. ½m out to sea is *Looe Island*, reached by ferry in the

summer. The island has its own fresh water, and once supported a population of Benedictine monks (the remains of their monastery can still be seen).

With so much fishing there are numerous excellent fish restaurants. Boats can be hired and there is a wide choice of boat cruises. 2m E is the *Monkey Sanctuary*, where Amazonian woolly monkeys live on trees in generous open enclosures. Their successful breeding has been hailed as a breakthrough in conservation.

The picturesque harbour-village of **Polperro* is 5m W.

Lostwithiel
3C

Small town on A390, 8m NE of St Austell. EC Wed

The name perhaps comes from Lost-in-the-wood: certainly it is a town that has not grown since the 12th c. when it was Cornwall's capital and only Stannary town (i.e. it had exclusive control of the tin mines). It was once a port, but after the river silted up its prosperity and growth were halted.

There are some lovely buildings, including the *Old Grammar School* of 1781 (in Queen Street), the 12th-c. *Duchy Palace*, once the administrative buildings of the county, in Quay Street, and the magnificent 14th-c. *Bridge* over the Fowey. **St Bartholomew's Church** is, however, the finest building in the town. Set in a delightful leafy churchyard, the church has a 110ft tower with a decorated octagonal lantern and spire. Lostwithiel was fiercely Royalist and when, in 1643, the Earl of Essex captured the town for the Parliamentarians, he quartered his horses in the church and put the prisoners in the tower. Two tried to hide in the belfry, and to dislodge them he used a barrel of gunpowder. He succeeded in his aim, but the damage can still seen today by the careful observer. The town *Museum* in Fore Street is most entertaining.

1m N is **Restormel Castle**, a magnificent circular keep started c. 1100 but mainly of the late 13th c. The Parliamentarians garrisoned the

Tintagel, Old Post Office

Padstow

Egyptian House, Penzance

castle in the Civil War, but were driven out by the Royalists in 1644. Seen from a distance the castle looks wonderfully romantic, and its ramparts afford superb views of the Fowey Valley.

3m N of the town is *Lanhydrock House*, a historic house and park in the possession of the National Trust. *Boconnoc*, 3m E, a fine classical 18th-c. mansion, is unfortunately not open to the public.

Madron   4C
Village on B3312, 2m NW of Penzance

A widespread parish which takes in many of Penwith's best-known Bronze and Iron Age monuments. Those doing a round tour of the peninsula can approach these antiquities from the N: Lanyon Quoit, for example, is midway between Madron and the B3306.

The village itself has a large granite-built church, **St Madernus** (an 1887 restoration by J.P. St Aubyn), whose monuments to the great local families recall the fact that Penzance was once a fishing village, part of Madron's parish, and this the mother church. There are old bench ends and a 7th-c. inscribed memorial stone set into the W wall of the S aisle. To the N of the village is *Madron's Well*, which has an altar and the remains of the chapel.

2m N of Madron, by the roadside, is **Lanyon Quoit**, a Neolithic chamber tomb *c.* 2000BC rebuilt in 1824 after a collapse. The 17ft capstone is supported by three 5½ft uprights: the whole was originally covered by a huge mound or barrow measuring 90ft x 40ft beneath which lay the cremated remains. 1m along the road to the W a sign indicates a footpath to **Men-an-Tol** and *Men Scryfa*. The first is a porthole stone (used as the entrance stone to a megalithic chamber tomb), the second an inscribed early Christian memorial stone (not to be confused with the prehistoric standing stones elsewhere). An immediate turning opposite signposted 'Chun Castle' leads in ¾m to farm buildings. From here there is a short ascent to the splendid Iron Age

hill fort of **Chun Castle**, protected by two concentric drystone walls, the outer 8ft thick, the inner 15-20ft thick. The two walls have separate, staggered entrances to confuse the attacker; further protection was provided by an outer ditch. The castle was occupied between *c.*200BC and *c.*500AD. To the W is **Chun Quoit**, formed of four slabs roofed by a 12ft square capstone. The remains of the barrow which covered it still surround the monument.

Manaccan   4A
Village off B3293. 10m SE of Helston

A village high on a hill overlooking the head of Gillan Creek, with a *Church* best known for the ancient fig tree growing out of the S wall near the tower. There is a lovely walk along the creek past the hamlet of *St Anthony in Meneage*, with its own small *Church* near the sea (said to have been built as a thank-offering by shipwrecked Normans) to the exposed Dennis Point (3m).

Marazion   4D
Village on S coast (A394). 3m E of Penzance

At the landward end of the peninsula which connects *St Michael's Mount* to land at low tide, Marazion has marvellous sandy beaches, the best to the W of the village. The village itself is not particularly attractive – consisting of one long straggling street opening out into the grandly named Square. There is a small garden which is the best place for photographing St Michael's Mount, and a small aquarium. Ferry services to the Mount operate at high tide.

At the *World of Entertainment* 1m E on the B3280 at Goldsithney is a family leisure park with a nostalgic theme: vintage amusements, mechanical music, old gramophones and magic lanterns.

Menheniot   3D
Village off A38, 3m SE of Liskeard

Although only 2m away from the A38, this pleasant village with its slate-roofed Georgian cottages is little visited. It is set in beautiful wooded countryside, much less spoilt than along the coast.

The village spreads out from an attractive central square dominated by the parish *Church*. The building is unusual for its spire (rare in Cornwall) but is otherwise a typical Cornish church, with a large S aisle and barrel roofs, not too zealously restored. The greatest pleasure of Menheniot is *The White Hart Inn*, a pub of great antiquity with an excellent cold table.

Mevagissey 3B
Village on S coast (B3273), 6m S of St Austell

The archetypal Cornish fishing village, with an inner and outer harbour and narrow streets and alleys rising steeply inland. In the 19th c. Mevagissey was a major fishing port with over 100 boats, catching millions of pilchards every year. They were salted and exported all over the world, but especially to the West Indies and Italy. In the Royal Navy salted pilchards (never a favourite with the ranks) were always known as 'Mevagissey Duck'. But with the depletion of the seas the industry declined and today there are only a handful of inshore fishing vessels and the once all-pervasive smell of fish has gone from the town.

The parish *Church*, now dedicated to St Peter but formerly to the Sts Mevan and Issey (hence Meva-gissey), is basically 12th- and 15th-c., but unfortunately was over-restored in the 19th c. It retains some good monuments, however, and a Norman font. In the old lifeboat station there is an interesting *aquarium* and in a boat-builder's workshop and yard of 1745 a lively *museum* of local crafts, agriculture and seafaring. In the heart of the village is a well-presented *model railway* with over 1000 models and a variety of layouts.

From the harbour, a cliff-top road connects the village with *Portmellon* (½m S), a delightful hamlet of cottages nestling around a good swimming beach. From the harbour there are boat-trips around the bay and boats may be hired for shark fishing, an activity almost as popular here as in Looe.

Minions see *St Cleer*

Morwenstow 1C
Village off A39, 8m N of Bude

Little more than a hamlet near the cliff-tops in northernmost Cornwall, Morwenstow owes its celebrity to the vicar who was here from 1843-75, the Anglo-Catholic Rev. Robert Hawker. Hawker was an eccentric who wrote poetry in a hut on the cliff, buried drowned sailors beneath a ship's figurehead in the churchyard, and built an odd vicarage with chimneys like church towers. He was, however, the man who brought the Harvest Festival into the church calendar – a more serious claim to fame.

The *Church of St Morwenna* retains some of its original Norman architecture in its fine S door and arcade to the N aisle. ½m S of Morwenstow is *Tonacombe*, a fine Tudor mansion (not open to the public).

There is a circular walk from Morwenstow along the cliffs. (See *Walk 1*, p.24.)

Mount Edgcumbe 3D
Historic house on B3247, 4m SW of Plymouth via Torpoint ferry or 1m by Cremyll passenger ferry

Magnificently placed on the Plymouth Sound, Mount Edgcumbe was the Tudor mansion of the Edgcumbe family (who also owned the medieval *Cotehele) until it was destroyed in 1941 during air-raids on Plymouth. Since the war it has been faithfully rebuilt but the interior, though open to the public, is not very interesting. It is the landscaped park with its wonderful views of Plymouth and The Sound that makes a detour worthwhile. In addition to 900 acres of mature woodland and 'English Parkland' with deer, there is a famous Italian garden, formal English garden, French garden and Orangery. There is a pleasant circular walk from the park around the peninsula overlooking the Sound. (See *Walk 7*, p.25.)

Mousehole 4C
Village on S coast off B3315, 4m S of Penzance
Event: Carnival (early Aug)

This is the village where tragedy struck three days before Christmas 1981, when 8 men on the Penlee lifeboat were drowned while trying to rescue seamen from a stricken cargo-boat. But with typical Cornish spirit, the *Penlee Lifeboat Station* (½m N of the harbour) is operating again, manned by volunteers. The station is normally open to the public on weekdays (9-5).

Mousehole itself is picturesque and charming, with a handful of narrow streets stretching outwards from the harbour. Once an important port, it never grew again after being destroyed by the Spanish in 1595 and has remained a small village. The harbour, which faces E, is normally sheltered (except in an easterly gale) by *St Clement's Isle* 300yds out to sea. This low rocky outcrop is popular with sea-birds but in storms waves break right over the top.

Mousehole does not have a church in the village. In a typically Cornish arrangement, the inhabitants were expected to walk 1m up a steep hill inland to **Paul** for their religious services. The **Church of St Pol de Leon** was founded by that saint in the 6th c. Nothing of the original church remains except a cross in the churchyard wall, at least 1000 years old. The next church was burnt to the ground by the Spanish during their raid of 1595. However, the 13th-c. tower survived, and one arch in the S aisle where the scorch-marks in the stone can still be clearly seen. The new (16th-17th-c.) church cannot have been so soundly built: the nave arches have a pronounced and alarming outwards lean. A real curiosity in the churchyard is the *Tomb of Dorothy Pentreath*, erected by Prince Louis Lucien Bonaparte, one of Napoleon's children. When she died in 1777, she was the 'last person who conversed in the ancient Cornish language'. With her it died in the parish of Paul.

Mullion   4A
Village on S coast (B3296), 5m N of Lizard Point

Mullion, though set amongst hills back from the sea, has the distinction of being surrounded by some of the best coastal scenery in the country. The village itself is nothing special, but the *Church* (c. 1500) has some of the very finest bench ends, dating from the reign of Henry VIII, representing the Passion, jesters, monks and animals.

Mullion Cove, the old harbour for the village, is a tiny inlet in the sheer serpentine cliffs. Protected by the National Trust, the cove has a small jetty, a few fishing boats and a handful of cottages. Near the coast, and acting as a natural breakwater as well as a perfect scenic backdrop, is *Mullion Island* (also NT), uninhabited except by thousands of breeding sea-birds. ¾m N is *Polurrian Cove*, a wider bay with a very good sandy beach. The only access is down a steep path.

2m N, reached only by the coastal path, is *Poldhu Point* with the *Marconi Monument*. This commemorates the transmission of the first telegraphic signal across the Atlantic in 1901. Although it seems improbable now, the world's first broadcast was made from this headland. Today all the workshops have gone and the land is owned by the National Trust.

Poldhu Cove just around the headland is a sandy beach (accessible by road) as is the next bay, *Church Cove*. Here is the unusual **Gunwalloe Church**, built almost on the beach against the cliffs with its detached belfry rising from them. Basically 13th-c. (S porch, aisle and tower) with 15th-c. additions (nave and chancel), the church is under continual threat of being washed away by the sea. The parish of *Gunwalloe* has a daunting history of shipwrecks, but so far little booty has been recovered from the sands.

Mylor   4A
Village off A39, 5m N of Falmouth

Once the smallest royal dockyard in the country, Mylor is now very popular with yachtsmen and has moorings for over 200 boats. There is a chandlery and a number of boat builders and repairers. The parish *Church*, beautifully situated by the entrance to the creek, makes a most rewarding composition with its unusual detached tower, but the interior is disappointing.

Newlyn 4C
Town on S coast (B3315), 2m SW of Penzance

Newlyn probably has less to do with tourism than any other town or village in Penwith (the toe of Cornwall). It has a busy working harbour for its fishing fleet and the largest fish-market in the south-west. The harbour is very colourful when the brightly painted inshore-fishing boats are in and the nets drying on the quay. The town has a cannery for pilchards and mackerel, so that Newlyn almost always smells fishy. Above the harbour are narrow alleys of small 19th-c. fishermen's cottages.

The *Newlyn Art Gallery* on the Penzance road has regular exhibitions of work by local artists. The beautiful little village of **Mousehole* is 3m S.

Newquay 3A/3B
Pop 13,890. On N coast 14m SW of Wadebridge (A3059), 16m NE of Redruth (A3075). Event: Carnival week (last in May). EC Wed. Inf: Tel (06373) 71345

Cornwall's major resort has every conceivable attraction, except peace and quiet: but that can readily be found elsewhere and this is the place for fun and activity. Foremost attraction is the coastline, with its five local beaches from Trevelgue to Towan Head and others to the W. The sand is firm and golden and almost limitless at low tide. The bay in which the town lies is protected by Towan Head, but bracing cliff-top walks can be enjoyed on both sides of the town and there are plenty of headlands, caves and inlets to explore. In the season the town itself is the liveliest in Cornwall, with everything from a variety theatre to outdoor discos; outside the town there is a wide choice of day or half-day outings.

The site of the town was settled as far back as the Bronze Age, but 'Towan Blistra' is first recalled as a fishing village in the 15th c., with a pier in the sheltered crook of the headland where the harbour now lies. Pilchards provided the main harvest, and a special lookout on Towan Head – the 'Huer' – proclaimed the arrival of the shoals through a special 4ft-long trumpet, bringing out the fisherfolk to haul in

Beach at Newquay

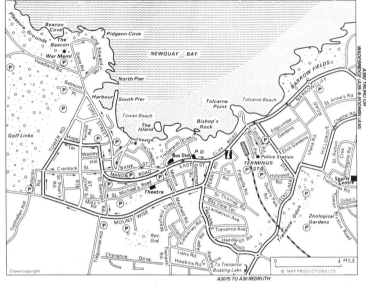

Crown copyright

A3075 TO A30 REDRUTH

© MAP PRODUCTIONS LTD

Newquay

━━━ **Through routes** ⟶ **One-way streets** Ⓟ **Parking**

and salt the catch. In the 19th c. the harbour was developed and a railhead established for the export of china clay, copper and iron ore. (Newquay has not been used as a port since the '20s and the old railway has gone; but the stone jetty where it terminated still lies in the middle of the harbour and the tunnel by which it passed through the cliff now houses an *aquarium*).

With the decline of the fishing and mining industries, tourism assumed increasing importance after the arrival of the railway (1875). The first visitors stayed at The Old Inn, in the oldest part of town. (Now *The Central Hotel* in Fore Street, the inn has a nostalgic collection of photos of old Newquay.)

Newquay's fine sandy **beaches** are among the best in Europe and range from the sheltered *Towan Beach* by the harbour (ideal for families) to the exposed *Fistral Beach* on the W side of Towan Head (for surfing). Three walks from the town offer splendid views of the coastal scenery. The first is to *Towan Head*, taking in the 150-year-old

Huer's Hut, the *lifeboat slipway* (1890s) and *Fistral Beach*. The second is to *Porth* and *Trevelgue Head*, the third to *Crantock, by crossing the River Gannel at Penpol (2½m).

Newquay's parish *Church of St Michael* was built in 1909, an early work of Ninian Comper. (The old parish church was at St Columb Minor.)

On Newquay's outskirts, a few minutes by car from the town centre, is the *Zoo and Leisure Park* of *Trenance Gardens*, with enough to keep the family happy for a day. Nearby is the attractive *Trenance Museum* of local history. 4m SE, on the A3058 at Tresillian Barton, is the fascinating *Dairyland*, a working farm and country life museum in which 160 cows are milked to music on a rotating milker – Europe's most advanced milking parlour.

3m SE of Newquay off the A3058 is **Trerice** (NT), a small manor house of 1571, home of the Arundell family. The grey limestone façade has two unusual features. The curved gables show a Dutch influence, unseen elsewhere in the West Country, which may result from the campaigns of the original owner, Sir John Arundell, in the Low Countries, and there is a splendid central window, two stories in height, with 24 lights and 576 panes. This window illuminates the splendid *Great Hall*, which has a contemporary plaster ceiling and fireplace. The plasterwork throughout the house is superb, and the house has excellent furniture, tapestries and clocks. Cream teas are served in the Barn restaurant.

5m S of Newquay off the A3075 at Newlyn East is the *Lappa Valley Railway*, a narrow gauge steam railway dating back to Victorian times. The miniature train offers a 2m return trip through attractive countryside.

Padstow   2B
Town 8m NW of Wadebridge (A389), 18m NE of Newquay (B3276). Event: Hobby Horse Celebrations (May 1). EC Wed. Inf: Tel (0841) 532296

On the S shore of the Camel estuary, this attractive old port is now extremely popular with visitors to Cornwall's N coast. It appeals especially to the sailing community, offering a haven from the rocky Atlantic coastline. But the sands of the estuary, such a splendid sight at low tide, also posed a continuing threat to shipping in the days when this was a waterway for the export of copper ore, slate and tin. The sandbar across the entrance to the estuary was rightly called the Doom Bar, and in the last century the Padstow lifeboat was one of the busiest in the country. Now in the summer months the estuary is alive with sailing dinghies, canoes and other small craft. Most of these are based on the sailing centre at *Rock* on the N side of the estuary (there is a regular passenger ferry to Rock from the harbour entrance at Padstow).

Padstow's narrow streets make parking very difficult, with only limited space on the quay. The best idea is to leave the car in the park above the town by the A389 and walk down. In the upper part of the town N of the car park is **St Petroc's Church**, whose name reminds us that this was the landing place of Cornwall's patron saint, the Irish St Petroc. St Petroc moved on to Bodmin, but the town took his name (Petroc-stow) and a monastery was founded here. The present church of the 15th c., restored 1850s, maintains a 14th-century tradition of worship on the site. It has some interesting details: a 15th-c. font of dark catacleuse slate from Harlyn Bay, carved with the figures of the apostles; a brass on the communion step of Laurence Merther, vicar at the time of the building of the church (1421); an ancient holy water stoop to the right of the altar with a carved figure of St Petroc; and an oak pew below it with a 15th-c. carved bench end depicting a fox in the pulpit preaching to a congregation of geese.

Uphill beyond the church is the imposing slate-built *Prideaux Place*, with castellated parapet and walls. This 16th-c. manor, with Georgian additions, is still the home of the Prideaux family who have done much to conserve the surroundings of the town. (Not open to the public.) Below the manor, in Fentonluna Lane, is Padstow's celebrated *Tropical Bird and Butterfly Gardens* – well worth a visit.

Padstow itself is centred on two picturesque quays connected by the short curve of Broad Street (small *museum* of local history). Each quay has a historic house: South Quay the 16th-c. *Raleigh's Court* where Sir Walter Raleigh held court when he was warden of Cornwall (not open to the public); North Quay the fascinating 15th-c. **Abbey House**, open to the public in summer. Sea food can be bought on the quay, and there are boat trips around the estuary. *The Harbour Inn* is a characteristic Cornish public house.

There are splendid walks around Padstow, and the footpath to Chapel Stile Field will take the walker on to the secluded *St George's Cove*. This walk can be extended to *Stepper Point* and *Trevone*, a distance of 11m. There is a beautiful walk from Padstow to *Wadebridge* along the Camel Estuary, following the course of the old railway line (5m, return by bus).

Paul see *Mousehole*

Pencarrow 2B/2C
Historic house off A389, 4m NW of Bodmin

This attractive Georgian mansion, a rebuilding (1776) of their old family home, is the property of the Molesworth-St Aubyn family. The Palladian S and E fronts are particularly impressive. Visitors are escorted round the house, which contains an excellent collection of 18th-c. furniture, china and paintings, including works by Reynolds. The grounds include an Italian garden, a giant rockery, a bog garden and palm house, which can be discovered by following marked trails. There is a children's corner, with peacocks and pets.

Pendeen 4C
Village on B3306, 3m N of St Just

Here is a village with a working mine, one of only four still producing tin in Cornwall. One of the shaft workings of **Geevor Mine** can be seen by the road outside the village, but the mine, registered in 1911, includes many older buildings in the vicinity. It reaches a depth of over 2000ft, much of it under the sea. Visitors to the mine are allowed to tour the treatment plant, and there is a museum showing the history of tin mining in the county.

The unusual **St John's Church** (1851) was designed by its vicar, who used Iona Cathedral as a model. 1m N of Pendeen is the lighthouse, *Pendeen Watch*, built in 1900 to protect shipping from the Wra Stones off the head. The lighthouse is open to the public on weekday afternoons.

Penryn 4A
Town on A39, 3m NW of Falmouth. Event: Town Fair (Aug Bank Hol)

Much older than Falmouth, and once much more important, Penryn received its charter in 1265 but lost its primacy as a port to its neighbour from the time of Elizabeth I. Today it is a charming quiet Georgian town, unspoilt by its main activity – the quarrying of granite.

The centre of the town is a wide street along the ridge of a hill above the Penryn River estuary. There are a number of grand buildings including the porticoed *Anchor Inn*, the *Teetotal Hall* of 1852, and grandest of all, the *Town Hall* (1825) with its bold clock tower. Many of the houses are much older than they look, having been refaced with granite façades in the 18th or 19th c., as visitors will discover if they explore the alleys off the main street which reveal the older and unsmartened backs of the buildings.

Penwith 4C
W Cornwall

The westernmost part of Cornwall and England; that part of the county W of the River Hayle. If Cornwall is England's foot, this is its toe. Sometimes known as the Cornishman's Cornwall because it is a distillation of all the strongest characteristics of the county, Penwith covers only a tiny area – it is little more than 15m wide and 6m N-S at its E end.

Penwith's position not only makes it the remotest part of Cornwall, but also the bleakest. It is all granite, with a central ridge of windswept moorland rising to 800ft. It takes the full force of Atlantic storms and the prevailing SW winds bend the stunted trees into weird shapes.

This tiny peninsula is richer in prehistoric remains than any other part of the country, having been extensively colonised by Bronze Age and Iron Age settlers. There were hill-top forts (*Castle-an-Dinas*, see *Chysauster*; *Chun Castle*, see *Madron*; and *Caer Bran* see *Sancreed*), and villages of primitive tin-workers and farmers. Two have been excavated and are extremely interesting (*Chysauster* and *Carn Euny* at *Sancreed*). The other prehistoric remains – and there are hundreds – include quoits, stone circles, standing stones and barrows: the physical remains of the burial of tribal chiefs and their unknown religion. For the best see *Lamorna*, *Madron*, *Sancreed* and *Zennor*.

Penwith has always had a much stronger Celtic (less Anglo-Saxon) character than the rest of Cornwall or England, and that despite Norman attempts to suppress the local saints. They failed, and the Cornish language survived in Penwith when natives E of the Hayle were speaking English. Dolly Pentreath, the last Cornish speaker, died in Paul (see *Mousehole) in 1777.

From prehistoric times to the beginning of this century, tin-mining was important in the peninsula, as the spectacular engine houses at *Botallack testify. But the sea has always been more important. The remote inaccessible coves, surrounded by high cliffs, often riddled with caves, were ideal for smuggling, and the appalling roads kept the Preventive Men away. The rocks off *Land's End and the inhospitable cliffs took a heavy toll of shipping, and consequently saw much wrecking. And fishing, especially from *Newlyn, was widespread, although it declined with the disappearance of the pilchards. Today the same villages, coves and bays attract thousands of visitors. See *Lamorna, *Mousehole, *Porthcurno, *St Ives and *Sennen.

See also Walk 3, p.24 and Motoring Tour 2, p.27.

Penzance   4C

Pop 19,360. 10m NE of Land's End (A30). Events: West Cornwall Spring Show (late Mar), Eve of St Peter & St John (Jun 28), EC Wed MD Thur & Sat. Inf: Tel (0736) 2341 & 2207

This is England's westernmost town, the start and end of the railway line, and (excluding the small town of Helston) it is also England's most southerly. As a result of this favoured position, and the climatic effects of the Gulf Stream, it has some of Britain's mildest weather. Plants grow here that are found nowhere else in Britain; it is the 'Montpelier of England'.

Penzance has a long history, although it was not incorporated until 1614. It appears in the Domesday Book and became a market town in 1332. In 1595 calamity struck. The Spanish, seeking revenge after the defeat of their Armada seven years earlier, attacked Newlyn, Mousehole and Penzance, burning all three to the ground. No old buildings

survived. The town was again destroyed in 1646 by the Parliamentarians, under General Fairfax, because the inhabitants had all been staunch Royalist supporters. When King Charles II came to the throne he rewarded the town with coinage rights (the weighing and assaying of tin), a privilege it retained for 200 years. Even then Penzance did not have peace: throughout the 17th c. it was troubled by marauding pirates from France, Algiers and Turkey. It was these less than entertaining raids which provided the inspiration for Gilbert and Sullivan's comic masterpiece – The Pirates of Penzance.

Despite the coinage rights and prosperous tin-mines in the area, Penzance remained a quiet market town until the coming of the railways (although its mild weather had made it popular with invalids in the Regency period). The railways brought the tourists and soon boarding houses, hotels and horse-drawn trips to Land's End began. Today Penzance depends on its tourist trade, although it is still an important port (and heli-port) for the Isles of Scilly, and has pilchard fishing and even a little international trade.

Penzance has the only true Promenade in Cornwall, facing SE across Mounts Bay towards the Lizard. At the N end, beyond the Jubilee bathing pond, is the harbour and dry dock. RMV Scillonian, the regular ferry to the Scillies, leaves from here.

The main streets of the town are Market Jew Street and Chapel Street. They meet at the centre of the town where the glorious Wren-style Market House (now a bank) complete with a dome (1837) is to be found. Sir Humphrey Davy, cast in bronze, stands in front facing down Market Jew Street. A Penzance man, he was not only the inventor of the miner's safety lamp which saved thousands of lives, but also a pioneering chemist, President of the Royal Society and a poet. Chapel Street is a beautiful curved street of 18th-19th-c. houses with good façades and excellent shops and restaurants at

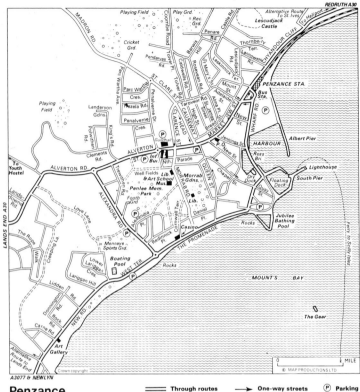

A3077 & NEWLYN

Penzance

═══ Through routes   **→ One-way streets**   **Ⓟ Parking**

ground floor level. The **Egyptian House** (NT) has one of the most remarkable façades of any town house. Built in 1835 during a brief craze for Egyptiana, the highly painted front resembles the entrance to a Pharaoh's temple.

The **Nautical Museum** further down Chapel Street has a full-size section of a 4-deck Man-o'-War of the 1730s, and shows the conditions in which the sailors had to live. There are also displays of treasure salvaged from local wrecks. The parish *Church* at the bottom of Chapel Street is a 'commissioners' church' of 1834, built in the Cornish idiom with a bold tower that has become an important landmark for sailors.

W of Chapel Street, the **Morrab Gardens** are unusual for their plants – aloes, myrtles, camelias and palms not normally found outdoors in England. The **Penlee House Museum** (Morrab Road) houses the town collections of local archeology, mining and history. Penzance's third museum, the **Geology Museum**, is housed in the Guildhall to the N (Alverton Street). Comprising the collections of the Royal Geological Society of Cornwall, it was founded in 1814 and is the second oldest geological museum in the world.

There is a tremendous amount to see in the area, which makes Penzance an excellent base for a holiday. *St Michael's Mount* (NT) is 3m E and *Trengwainton House Gardens* (NT) 2m

NW. *Newlyn is 1m SW and has a busy working harbour. Beyond it is *Mousehole and a string of beautiful villages and coves before *Land's End, only 10m away. Penzance is also an ideal centre for exploring the antiquities (quoits, standing stones, etc.) of the Penwith peninsula (see *Madron) and the tin mines of the W coast (*Botallack, *Pendeen). Excellent beaches lie to the S (Newlyn) and E (Marazion).

British Airways operate several helicopter flights daily from the Heliport, Penzance to the **Isles of Scilly** (not Sun). Tel (0736) 3871. A daily steamship service also operates from Penzance to St Mary's (winter 2-3 times weekly). Tel (0736) 2009/4013.

Perranporth 3A
Village on N coast (B3284/B3285), 11m SW of Newquay

A copper-mining centre in the early 19th-c., Perranporth was much built up after the war, the by-product of the 2m of splendid beach to the N, backed by the sweeping dunes of Penhale Sands. Relics of the industrial past are seen in the course of the old railway, the disused mines and 19th-c. slate cottages. Another interesting relic is, unfortunately, no longer visible, but worth mentioning here. This is the tiny **Oratory of St Piran**, the oldest known Christian church in the country, isolated among the sand dunes 2m N of Perranporth. Founded in the 6th c. by the Irish missionary St Piran, the oratory was buried by drifting sand in the 11th c. and only revealed in the early 19th c. To preserve the structure, which incorporates a Norman doorway, the oratory has been reburied. After the oratory had been abandoned a later church (1150) was built further inland, but this was also buried and a third church had to be built. The site was Perranzabuloe, 2m SE of Perranporth: this last church was erected in 1804.

St Piran, the patron saint of tin miners, is commemorated in two other places: Perranwell, site of the ancient St Piran's Well, and St Piran's Round. The latter lies 1m E of Perranporth near Rose and 30yds off the B3285. A natural amphitheatre 130ft in diameter, it is said that Cornish miracle plays were performed here.

Popular sports at Perranporth include surfing, sand-yachting, and gliding, the latter operated by the local Cornish Gliding and Flying Club.

Perranporth

Polperro 3C

Village on S coast (A387), 6m W of Looe

Located at the foot of a plunging valley on Cornwall's rocky S coast, this is a magical place, one of the most romantic of all seaside villages. Unfortunately it suffers for its beauty in the high season with thousands of visitors, although tourists' cars are now forbidden entry. Despite the overcrowding, Polperro should not be missed. It is a small village of diminutive white-washed slate cottages, scattered in tiny streets around the harbour. On the E side of the quay a retired fisherman has added a charming touch to one of the cottages, embedding its front with shells.

Until this century the very steep valley was impassable except on horseback, and so in former times the main industry of the village was smuggling. Almost every cottage has a cellar or secret hiding hole and vast quantities of brandy, tea, lace and diamonds found their way into Cornwall despite the efforts of the Preventive Men. The tradition continues: the successful 'Operation Cyril' in 1979 caught smugglers unloading £6 million worth of drugs into Talland Bay 1m E of the village. Indeed, as the judge sagely pronounced while sentencing the gang, 'this was exactly the sort of place chosen for centuries as being ideal for their purposes'. The *Museum of Smuggling* tells the full story on the harbour.

The *Land of Legend* and *Model Village* in the heart of Polperro has 'animated models and Cornish traditions' and a scale model of Polperro. There are also numerous restaurants, gift shops and pubs.

Polruan see *Fowey*

Pool see *Camborne*

Porthcurno 4C

Village on S coast off B3315, 4m SE of Land's End

On any excursion to Land's End, a detour should be made to Porthcurno. It has an exceptionally lovely *beach*, perhaps Cornwall's finest. Apart from the temperature of the water it could be on a Greek island. There are two beautiful heather and bracken-covered headlands, between which is a steep white sandy beach and absolutely clear blue water.

Porthcurno is also the improbable headquarters of 'Cable and Wireless Engineering College – Worldwide Communications', and the terminal point of 11 ocean cables, the earliest of which is the England-Bombay cable of 1870. On the W headland above the beach (road access) is the **Minack Theatre**, founded in 1932 with a season every summer since then. It is a Greek-style theatre using the natural slope of the cliffs and rock formations to provide the stage and auditorium. Seats are cut in the slope. Whatever the standard of the plays there can be no more beautiful backdrop than Porthcurno Bay, the *Logan Rock* headland opposite and the sea. (Open to visitors most summer afternoons.)

From Minack Theatre the road leads on to *St Levan*. Here is another lovely beach (reached by a steep path). Overlooking the beach are the ruined remains of a holy oratory and well. The road ends at **St Levan's Church**, a beautifully remote church with wonderful woodwork. The Tudor screen is very fine and the bench ends exceptional. In addition to the usual motifs of animals, fish and jesters are a number of portraits, believed to be of 15th-c. parishioners. They are carved with enormous care and expression. The font is at least 850 years old. The churchyard has two Celtic crosses, one 7ft high. By the W tower is a communal pit-grave to 23 men lost in the shipwreck *Khyber* in 1905. It is only one of a number of graves of people lost at sea.

Porthleven 4A

Village on S coast (B3304), 3m SW of Helston

A small working harbour used by fishermen and crabbers. To the E of the village extend the *Porthleven* and *Loe Sands*, two miles of unbroken beaches. Because there is no road access they are entirely undeveloped and in the morning and late evening – even in August – they are deserted. Behind the *Loe Bar*, near the centre of the beach is **The Loe**, Cornwall's largest natural lake formed by the drifting sands and shingle. There are lovely walks along its E shore (National Trust) through cedarwoods and parkland, and it is a haven for birdwatchers. Until the beginning of this century, the bar was regularly cut through to lower the level of the lake when flooding threatened Helston at its top end. Just to the E is a tragic memorial to 100 men killed when the warship *Anson* was wrecked on the beach in 1807. The men were all buried in a mass pit on the site. The disaster inspired Henry Trengrouse to create his patent rocket-firing life-saving apparatus which has subsequently saved thousands of lives. (See also *Walk 4*, p.24.)

Porthtowan 3A

Village on N coast off A30, 4m N of Redruth

An excellent sandy beach, one of the best in Cornwall, and magnificent walking country, make this an ideal small resort, suited for those in search of quiet. A lovely walk is to *Chapel Porth* along the beach, returning by the cliff or *vice versa*, depending on the tide. The valley inland from Porthtowan shows considerable evidence of the 19th-c. copper boom.

Port Isaac 2B

Village on N coast (B3267), 12m W of Camelford

Pitched precipitously against the sides of its valley, this small fishing village looks down on a sandy inlet, the Haven. Some of the narrow alleys between the slate-hung cottages are just wide enough for two people to pass (one is called Squeeze Belly Alley!). There is still some lobster-fishing, and the 'Bloody Bones' bar of the splendid inn on the quayside is rigged out with lobster pots. This is an exceptionally rugged part of the coast, with majestic cliff walks. To the E is *Port Gaverne* and to the W *Port Quin*, once used – like Port Isaac – for the shipping of slate from the nearby quarry at *Delabole*.

Portloe 3B

Village on S coast off A3078, 14m SW of St Austell

Perhaps because the harbour is so forbidding and the approach so difficult, or perhaps because it is so small, Portloe is one of the most unspoiled Cornish coastal villages. It has an old pub, *The Ship Inn*, and a small hotel, but otherwise nothing to offer the visitor except black cliffs and whitewashed cottages perched precariously along the road down to the small slipway. An exciting place in a storm.

Port Quin 2B

Inlet on N coast off B3314, 14m W of Camelford

A tiny beach, slipway and a few cottages are relics of an abandoned slate and fishing port. In the late 19th c. all the men of the village were drowned at sea and the women moved out. *Doyden Point*, preserved by the National Trust, has an early 19th-c. folly in the 'Gothick' style. There is a bracing walk to *Port Isaac* E across the cliffs.

Portreath 3A

Village on N coast (B3300), 4m N of Redruth

Originally a small fishing port, Portreath was developed in the late 18th c. as a dock. The idea was to ship in coal for the local mines and ship out the ore for smelting. The man behind the project was Lord de Dunstanville, one of the local Bassett family of landowners. Although the harbour was put to good use for 200 years there were too many shipwrecks at the narrow entrance between the pier and the cliff, and along the coastline to the W.

Today the 18th-c. pier, the relics of a 1-in-10 inclined railway up from the docks and some workmen's cottages all record Portreath's industrial past: now it is a holiday retreat with a sandy beach (good surfing).

There are splendid walks in either direction on the Cornwall North Coast Path: E along the cliffs to *Porthtowan* (5½m) or W to *Godrevy* at the E end of St Ives Bay (8m). The latter walk offers many natural features: coves, cliffs and the haunts of sea birds and seals.

Portscatho 4B
Village on S coast off A3078, 12m SE of Truro

An exposed village facing E onto the sea with fine views to Nare Head and Gull Rock (4m E) across the bay. There is an attractive row of small Georgian cottages known as *The Lugger* above the jetty. Although the small harbour is rocky (and consequently treacherous at low tide) there is a sandy beach at the N end of the village (Porthcurnick Beach). This whole stretch of coast is largely unvisited and remarkably unspoilt.

Poughill 1C
Village off A39, 1m N of Bude

St Olaf's Church (14th-c.) is well worth a visit. The best features here are the beautifully carved bench ends, the oldest 15th-c., and the barrel roofs of the same period with their carved wooden bosses. In the N aisle are the royal arms of Charles II in plaster relief (seen also at Stratton) commemorating the support given by Poughill to the Royalist cause in the Civil War. The unusual medieval wall paintings were re-coloured in 1894.

Probus 3B
Village on A390, 5m NE of Truro

St Probus's Church is distinguished by the tallest and finest tower in the county (125ft). Built in the Perpendicular style in 1523, it has two tiers of very delicate pierced stone screens. Although 'restored' in Victorian times, the interior is also good. The tower is separated from the body of the church with a Tudor wooden screen with the letters ABCDE painted on, suggesting that it was once used as the village school. The screen separating the sanctuary from the nave is also of excellent workmanship, and the sanctuary is covered in Victorian mosaics.

Just to the E of the village is the **County Demonstration Garden** with over 50 permanent displays illustrating all aspects of practical gardening from fruit growing to compost techniques. There are also guided tours, special lectures 1st Sunday of each month) and advisors available for consultation on Thursday afternoon. A must for gardeners.

1m further E is **Trewithen**, a lovely 18th-c. 'classical box' lived in continuously by the same family since it was built. There are guided tours around the house, which has fine furniture and pictures (including a Reynolds portrait). But it is the 20 acres of gardens, laid out with the house, that most people come for. The magnolias, rhododendrons and camelias are famous and there are rare shrubs, trees and a lake. The rest is mature parkland.

Prussia Cove 4D
S coast bay off A394, 8m E of Penzance

A beautiful sandy beach surrounded by cliffs riddled with caves, reached only by a 3/4m walk and a steep ladder, and therefore completely uncommercialised. The bay derives its name from the most notorious of the Cornish smugglers, John Carter, who styled himself after his boyhood hero, the King of Prussia. The bay was ideal for his purposes, inaccessible by road but with numerous caves for storage. Nevertheless he protected his interests with a battery of guns along the cliff-tops! The cove has not been so accommodating to all its visitors. In 1947 the naval frigate *HMS Warspite* was beached broadsides in the bay on her way to the wreckers. She never reached her destination but was broken up when tugs tried to pull her off the rocks.

Redruth 3A
Pop 10,785. 17m NE of Penzance, 10m W of Truro (A30). EC Thur MD Fri

Redruth is a good deal older than its neighbour Camborne, and the many Georgian and early Victorian buildings testify to its former prosperity as Cornwall's tin mining centre. Since Camborne became the administrative centre, however, the old *Town Hall* (1850) has become unknown to the locals. It is now the Redruth Club and is located at the foot of the hill below the station in Penryn Street, near the splendid *railway viaduct* (1844). Joining Penryn Street is Cross Street, where stands the house of Redruth's most famous resident, *William Murdock*. Murdock was a pioneer mining engineer who invented gas lighting, and his house was the first in the world to be gas-lit (1792). Up the hill (Fore Street) is an impressive granite *clock tower* (1828 and 1904) in the Italian style. Redruth has many fine Nonconformist chapels, the most striking the Wesleyan Chapel of 1826 at the top of the hill.

The parish *Church of St Uny* is some way outside the centre of the town to the S, on the slopes of *Carn Brea*. This is a Georgian building of 1756, with a 15th-c. tower.

1m N of Redruth on the road to Portreath (B3300) is the **Tolgus Tin Mill**, used for processing waste from tin mines. It has been working for over 200 years and is now the only surviving tin mill in operation in the country. Visitors can tour the mill and see the streaming (separation of the ore). There is a good mineral shop and a children's play area.

Another industry near Redruth open to the public is *Foster's Pottery*, on the Redruth by-pass. Redruth's neighbouring town of *Camborne* has a lot of mining history, and 2m to the SE is the extraordinary *Gwennap* Pit, where John Wesley preached.

Restormel Castle see *Lostwithiel*

Roche 3B
Village off A30, 8m SW of Bodmin

The village itself is not remarkable but ¾m SE, signposted from the B3274, is *Roche Rock*, an extraordinary granite outcrop 100ft high, reminiscent of the Dartmoor tors. Perched on top are the ruined remains of **St Michael's Chapel**, built in 1409. This inhospitable pile of rocks was the home of a leper-hermit who survived on the food left for him at the bottom by local villagers. He lived underneath the tiny chapel (10 x 22ft) of which the granite walls but no floor or ceiling remains. From the top (reached by iron ladders) are good views all round, including the china-clay spoil heaps to the S and E.

Rock 2B
Village off B3314 7m NW of Wadebridge, 1m from Padstow via passenger ferry

A bungalow village on the N side of the Camel estuary, remarkable for its magnificent unspoiled sands. A centre for sailing, Rock is also noted for its fine golf course. To its N is the small Norman and 15th-c. **Church of St Enodoc**, with an unusual broached spire antedating the more familiar Cornish tower. This church, once almost lost in the drifting sand dunes, was retrieved by excavation in 1863 (part of a J.P. St Aubyn restoration). E of the golf course is *Jesus Well*, whose waters were once believed to cure whooping cough. A stone baptistery was built over it. A circular walk around Pentire Head, 3m N, offers some of the best N coast views. (See *Walk 2*, p.24.)

Ruan Minor 4A
Village off A3083, 5m NE of Lizard Point

An inland village adjacent to some of Cornwall's wildest and least accessible coastal scenery. The tiny *Church* (15th-c.) is in an exposed windswept position and from it starts a varied 3m circular *Nature Trail* through valleys and along the shore.

Poltesco (owned by the NT) 1m N is a small village which, remote and unvisited, shelters in a rocky gorge. *Kennack Sands* (1½m N of Ruan Major) are noted for their silvery grey sand. See also *Cadgwith*.

St Agnes 3A
Town on N coast (B3277), 11m NW of Truro, 7m N of Redruth

This was once one of Cornwall's most extensive mining areas, with something like 35 tin and copper mines employing 1000 miners. In 1840 at the height of the boom, St Agnes parish had a population of 8000: now it is only 5000. The mining declined in the early part of this century but the evidence of its activity is seen in ruined mine workings in the vicinity of the town and on the cliff-tops. The oldest part of St Agnes (Church Town) has the *Church of St Agnes* (1849) with a spire. The village is built on a steep hill and the row of cottages known as

'Stippy Stappy' on a footpath leading from the church down to the floor of the combe is built in steps. Opposite the lych gate of the church an alley leads up to 16th-c. cottages owned by the National Trust. Here is the excellent *St Agnes Pottery*.

The main beach in St Agnes is at *Trevaunance Cove* (sand and pebble), sheltered by St Agnes Head. Nearby are the granite blocks of the ruined quay rebuilt several times over the last three centuries but always destroyed by the sea. Other sand beaches are at *Chapel Port* (NT) and *Porthtowan*, both to the SW.

The cliff walks in the locality are superb, particularly in the spring. Best is to *St Agnes Head* and on to *Chapel Porth* past the *Wheal Coates Engine House* (NT), perched halfway down the cliff. To the N is the attractive area of *Perranporth* and the *Pendale Sands*. Inland, a footpath leads from the town to *St Agnes Beacon* (NT), which at 630ft offers a view stretching from Trevose Head in the N to St Ives in the W: from it one can see no less than 32 church towers.

On the S outskirts of the town (B3277) is the *St Agnes Leisure Park*, with landscaped gardens showing 'Cornwall in Miniature', model dinosaurs, children's amusements etc.

St Austell

3B
Pop 18,500. 14m NE of Truro (A390). EC Thur
MD Tue

St Austell is the capital of the English china-clay or kaolin industry. William Cookworthy discovered how to make true porcelain using kaolin, thus reviving a lost Chinese art, in 1768. Josiah Wedgwood followed quickly and began quarrying the area. Today miles of land to the N and W of the town are covered in clay pits and enormous spoil heaps. The kaolin is exported all over the world and used for much more than just porcelain, for example toothpaste, cosmetics, medicine and shiny 'art' paper. St Austell is the centre for this huge industry. Consequently although it is an excellent shopping town it is not an attractive place. It has large multi-storey car-parks and offices for the china-clay companies and few buildings more than 100 years old. Honourable exceptions are the *Quaker Meeting House* of 1829 near the station, *The White Hart Hotel* of c. 1800 near the church and the large 2-storey stone *Market House* with an exotic wood roof of 1791.

Holy Trinity Church is, however, much older, dating back to the Middle Ages when St Austell was a small tin-mining village. With its wonderful carved Perpendicular tower of 1487, the church must have seemed enormous when newly built. Other features of interest include the Norman font (modern canopy) and the late Norman Chapel of St Michael. The church was restored in the late 19th c.

St Austell's port is 2m SE at **Charlestown**. There was nothing here until the harbour was built in 1791 by Charles Rashleigh (who named the village after himself). A small harbour and larger lock were built with cottages around. In 10 years the population of the area grew from 10 to around 300. It has not grown much since, and so, although the harbour is still used by china-clay boats, it remains a lovely unspoilt Georgian village. Its qualities have been appreciated by film-makers: parts of *Poldark* and *The Voyage of Charles Darwin* were made here. There is an excellent hotel and a first-rate pub (*The Rashleigh Arms*) but the greatest attraction is the **Shipwreck Museum and Visitors' Centre**, with models, objects salvaged from wrecks and a fascinating collection of photographs of stranded ships.

2m E of Charlestown is *Carlyon Bay*, a beautiful white sandy bay backed by high cliffs which is the site of *Cornish Leisure World*, a complex of roller skating, miniature railway, crazy golf, cafes, disco and dance halls with parking for 2,500 cars.

The *Wheal Martyn Museum*, which explains the history of the china-clay workings, is 2m N of St Austell on the A391.

St Breward   2C
Village on Bodmin Moor off B3266, 10m NE of
Bodmin

E of the River Camel on the edge of
Bodmin Moor, this village lies in an area
of considerable prehistoric activity.
Stone circles, the temples of Stone Age
man, and later Bronze Age hut circles
are dotted around the empty marshes to
the E. Most impressive is *King Arthur's
Hall*, a rectangular enclosure 159 x 60ft,
with earthbanks up to 20ft wide and 7ft
high, with a retaining wall of large
stones. Iron Age Celts followed and
there are traces of their huts and hill
forts. The two highest tors on Bodmin
are in the parish: *Brown Willy* (1377ft)
and *Rough Tor* (1311ft). These are best
approached from *Camelford*.

Originally Norman, the 15th-c.
Church was over-restored in 1864.

St Buryan   4C
Village on B3283, 6m E of Land's End

St Buryan's Church was founded in the
10th c. King Athelstan, resting in the
village before sailing to subjugate the
Isles of Scilly, vowed to found a church
if his mission was successful. He conq-
uered the islands and on his return
(932 AD) endowed the church. Because
the living (i.e. appointment of the
clergy) remained a 'Royal Peculiar' the
local bishop took no interest in the
church and for 550 years from 1301 only
two deans actually resided in the village.
As a result of this sorry arrangement the
old church fell into total disrepair and
a new one had to be built in the 15th c.
(the tower is 14th-c.). Further neglect
necessitated extensive restoration in the
last century. The 15th-c. rood screen – a
magnificent piece of workmanship –
survives and there is a Celtic cross in the
churchyard. Another dating from the
8th c. stands on an 18th-c. plinth in
front of the churchyard.

St Cleer   2C
Village on Bodmin Moor off B3254, 2m N of Liskeard

The largest parish on Bodmin Moor,
embracing farm and moorland and
many of E Cornwall's most celebrated
ancient monuments. The hamlets of the
parish mainly sprang up in the first half

of the 19th c. as a result of the copper-
mining boom. The demise of this
industry, at the end of the century, is
mourned by the stark ruins of the mine
workings on the moor to the NE. New
housing estates are, however, bringing
new life to the area.

The **Church of St Cleer** has a fine
15th-c. granite tower. Originally
Norman, the church has been much
altered. An illustration of this is in the
different columns of the nave arcades.
The octagonal piers of granite were
constructed when the N aisle was added
in the 14th c.: the polyphant stone piers
of the other arcade came with the
addition of the S aisle in the 15th c. The
woodwork of the barrel vaults is also
15th-c. The church was restored in
1904. The most unusual feature is the
series of 17th-c. wooden text boards
around the walls; unique in Cornwall.
These have been recently restored, as
has the Queen Anne coat of arms. E of
the church, 200yds down the hill, is a
holy well with a 15th-c. baptistery.

1m NW of St Cleer beside the road to
St Neot is **King Doniert's Stone**. Two
granite monoliths are maintained by the
Department of the Environment: one
the shaft of a Celtic cross (the cross is
missing), the other a stone inscribed
(invisibly) in Latin and dedicated to the
Cornish king Doniert (d. 875). Just S of
Darite, a village 1m E of St Cleer, is
Trethevy Quoit, a fine example of a
Bronze Age megalithic chamber tomb
(*c.* 1800BC). One of the supporting
stones has collapsed, causing the
capstone to tilt: otherwise the
monument is intact and an unusual
sight in this part of Cornwall.

At *Minions*, a hamlet 2½m NE of St
Cleer, a track leads off the road to **The
Hurlers**, a group of three Bronze Age
stone circles. Varying in diameter from
110-135ft, the circles had an obscure
religious purpose: a popular legend
suggests that they were a group of
villagers turned to stone for playing the
ancient game of hurling on a Sunday.
Past the fork in the road a little further
on, another path leads in 1m to the
Moor's most photographed landmark,

The Cheesewring. There is no credible explanation for this extraordinary formation of granite boulders piled on top of one another like loaves of bread. The climb to the hill (1250ft) is rewarded on a clear day by one of Cornwall's finest views. To the N are the tors, dotting the sweep of moorland with the highest point at Brown Willy to the NW. A circular walk of 7½m taking in the Cheesewring and the Hurlers is described on p.25 (*Walk 10*).

To the SE of Minions lies *Caradon Hill*, topped by its TV mast, which was the site of the discovery of copper in 1837. Ruined engine houses and closed-off shafts now scatter the area. Much of Devon and Cornwall and the two seas are also in view. In the village is a pub which at 995ft above sea level is the 'Highest Pub in Cornwall'.

St Clether   2C
Village off A395, 10m W of Launceston

Worth a mention for its *holy well*, enclosed by a chapel, the largest in Cornwall. The well is a pleasant ¼m walk along the River Inny W of the village. The river is little more than a stream here, but well-known for its trout. At the holy well the water passes from a well-head through the chapel: both buildings are 15th-c., restored in 1895. (The key to the chapel can be obtained from the church in St Clether.)

St Columb Major   3B
Town on A39, 9m SW of Wadebridge. Events: Hurling Competition (Shrove Tue & following Sat). EC Wed MD Mon

Bypassed by the A39, this town is rarely visited by tourists except during the annual hurling competition. The sport, here a cross between Rugby football and Irish hurling, is played with a wooden ball in a silver covering, following a tradition of at least 400 years.

The town has some distinctive Victorian buildings in vari-coloured brick and stone, and an imposing 15th-c. church, **St Columba**, with a large tower. The church has tombs and brasses commemorating the Arundells of Lanherne: one brass, to Sir John Arundell (1545) is probably the finest in

Cornwall. In the valley N of the town is the former rectory, a moated building by G.E. Street (1855), now a guest house. The building contains examples of Street's own furniture and ironwork.

3m N of the town on the edge of the marshy St Breock Downs in a field beside the road, are the *standing stones* known as 'The Nine Maidens', with another, 'The Fiddler' nearby. 2m E of the town on a prominent hill (Castle Downs, 705ft) is **Castle-an-Dinas**, a large Iron Age fort. Reached most quickly by footpath from Providence Farm, the circular fort has three protective ramparts and an elaborate entrance on the SW. The inner circle of the fort measures about 1700 x 1500ft and would have enclosed a complex of barracks, stables, granaries, etc., sufficient to maintain a large army.

Castle-an-Dinas is popularly believed to have been King Arthur's hunting lodge: he is reputed to have stayed here with his fellow knights while hunting wild deer on Tregoss Moor.

St Germans   3D
Village on B3249, 10m SE of Liskeard. Event: Elephant Fayre (last weekend in Jul)

A lovely village on the St Germans River, one of the remoter tributaries of the Tamar. Although the village is full of fine stone cottages and the six gabled 17th-c. *almshouses* are extremely pretty, it is the church for which it is deservedly famous.

St Germans Church was probably founded as a priory church in the 5th c. in honour of that saint (Germanus of Auxerre) – noted for his ferocious opposition to heresy. But its period of great glory was from 937 to 1049, when it was the seat of the Bishop of Cornwall, established by Athelstan. (After 1050 it was replaced by Exeter, which became the seat of a vast diocese covering the whole SW peninsula.) By the 12th c. the demoted Saxon church was in decay, and it was rebuilt by the Normans as the church of an Augustinian priory (since demolished). The W front has a magnificent Norman doorway with pillars and zig-zag decoration – one of the finest in the country. The two W towers are built on Norman bases, the octagonal one in the 13th c., the square one in the 15th. Inside, the church is impressively large, with a S aisle of equal size to the nave. The E window has stained glass by Burne-Jones and other windows in the chancel and S chapel are by William Morris & Co. The S chapel has monuments to the local Eliot family, and there is a fine statue of Edward Eliot by Rysbrack (1722) by the N tower, showing him in a Roman costume, reclining. The font is Norman.

Next to the church is *Port Eliot*, the castellated mansion of the Eliot family, who still live here. This stands on the site of the old priory house, purchased by the family in 1575. The present building was largely the work of the Regency architect Sir John Soane (not open to the public).

The *Elephant Fayre* is an ambitious off-beat fringe festival of theatre, music, dance and whole-food stalls.

St Ives
4C/4D

Town on N coast, (A3074/B3306) 10m N of Penzance. Event: Festival of Music & the Arts (Sep). EC Thur. Inf: Tel (0736) 796297

The virtue of St Ives is that for a place so celebrated as the essential Cornish seaside town, and an artists' colony *par excellence*, it has held on to so much of its original charm. One reason could be the restriction on visitors' cars, which cannot go into the town but must park above it; the rationing of tourist shops to one principal street, out of sight of the harbour; or perhaps the simple determination of the people of St Ives to keep it that way.

The beaches – Newquay's rolling sands on a smaller scale – are a further inducement to the holidaymaker: *Porthmeor* to the W of the Head, *Porthminster* to the S. The harbour, with the long *Smeaton's Pier* (1770) built by the architect of the Eddystone Lighthouse, now encloses a sand beach. Originally, when St Ives was a fishing village, it had a more significant role. Unfortunately, like Newquay, St Ives suffered from the departure of the pilchards and other fish from the area. The new resource turned out to be the town itself, with its colour-washed cottages and cobbled streets winding down to the harbour. The artists who came here in the wake of the railway (1877) set up their easels and established a tradition that is maintained to this day, not only by the weekend painters but by professional local groups.

Two artists indelibly identified with St Ives were the master potter Bernard Leach (d. 1979) and the sculptress Dame Barbara Hepworth (d. 1975). The *Leach Pottery*, now run by his widow Janet, is on Higher Stennack, the road into the town: the *Barbara Hepworth Museum and Sculpture Gallery* (administered by the Tate Gallery) is just off the main street (Fore Street) on Barnoon Hill in the heart of the town.

The 15th-c. **St Ives Church** (Church of St Ia) overlooking the harbour, has a majestic tower of Cornish granite shipped here from Zennor. Inside, the arcades, leaning outwards slightly, are made of sandstone. The finely carved ribs and bosses of the barrel roof have been recently painted and gilded to bring out their detail. Other interesting features in the church are the 15th-c. bench ends and granite font of the same period. The stylised, modernistic treatment of the carving of the font finds an echo (500 years on) in the beautiful Madonna and Child in the Lady Chapel, by Dame Barbara Hepworth. Carved out of smooth white stone, the sculpture was given to the church by Dame Barbara in memory of her son, killed on active service in the RAF. The stainless steel candleholders on the chapel altar were also her gift.

In Fore Street an unusual museum, opened in 1963, has proved a great success: the *Barnes Museum of Cinematography*. This private collection covers the evolution of moving pictures from the primitive shadow show to the invention of cinematography. Displays of works by St Ives' current artists can be seen in the upper, N part of the town

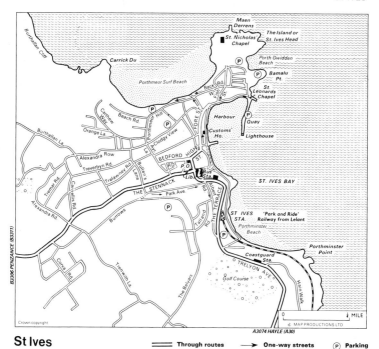

St Ives

=== Through routes   → One-way streets   Ⓟ Parking

St Ives Harbour

at the *Penwith Art Gallery* (Back Road West) and the *St Ives Society of Artists* in a former chapel in Norway Square.

A short walk may be made to the headland (*The Island*) N of the harbour, crowned by the rebuilt *Chapel of St Nicholas*. A longer one is from the railway station up Trelyon Hill to *Tregenna Castle* (1774), now a hotel, and thence to *Knills Monument*, a granite pyramid of 1782 commemorating an ex-mayor (and smuggler!) of St Ives. There is also Hain Walk, running E of the town to *Carbis Bay*, continuing with the Cliff Walk to *Lelant*.

St Juliot 2C
Village off B3263, 3m E of Boscastle

An almost uninhabited parish by the River Valency. Famous for the **Church of St Juliot**, associated with the novelist Thomas Hardy. Hardy restored the church in 1872 and in doing so met his first wife. The nave has a single aisle on the N, separated from it by a granite arcade. Memorials to Hardy and his wife are on the wall of the N aisle.

St Just (Penwith) 4C
Small town on B3306/A3071, 6m N of Land's End

The most westerly mainland town in England, whose former prosperity is declared by its solid granite houses and public buildings, notably the former Market House of 1840, now the *Wellington Hotel*. There is a fine *Methodist Chapel* (1833 and 1860) in the triangle at the centre of the town, and off the adjacent square is a grassy amphitheatre, the *Plain-an-Gwarry*, the setting of medieval Cornish plays and later on the preachings of Charles and John Wesley. Wrestling and mining competitions also took place here – the granite blocks on the green were used for drilling contests. The tinners, who worked *Botallack* and other local mines, were a tough, hard-drinking lot and it says much for the impact of the Wesleys that by 1750 St Just had Cornwall's largest Methodist Society.

Between St Just and Sennen is Land's End Airport, from which pleasure trips are flown along the coast.

St Just-in-Roseland 4B
Village on A3078, 12m S of Truro (via King Harry Ferry)

On a creek off Carrick Roads, St Just-in-Roseland is best known for its church and especially for the **churchyard**, acclaimed as the most beautiful in the country.

The churchyard, better described as a large sacred garden, is filled with hydrangeas, bamboos, palms, myrtles, magnolias, trees and flowers. Only in the area around the church are there any gravestones, but from everywhere there are glimpses through the foliage of the green hills over the creek. The *Church of St Just* itself, beautifully positioned at the waterside, was founded in 1261. The chancel and transept are from this date; the nave and S aisle about a century later.

St Keverne 4A
Village on B3293, 8m S of Falmouth

A large granite village 1½m inland from the inhospitable E coast of the Lizard Peninsula. The *Church* (founded 1266) is most unusual for its octagonal spire, rebuilt in 1770. This was an important landmark for sailors to Falmouth trying to avoid the infamous *Manacles* out to sea. All but one of these submarine rocks are covered at high tide and countless ships have gone down on them. Over 400 drowned sailors are buried in the churchyard.

NE of St Keverne are two attractive coves, accessible by car, at *Porthallow* and *Porthoustock*. See also *Coverack*.

Goonhilly Downs, which lie to the W of the village and are best seen from the B3293, are a flat plateau of serpentine rock. The serpentine is very hard and infertile, and the soil is rich in magnesium. Consequently rare plants of great interest to botanists grow on the open heathland which are not found elsewhere. The *Post Office Satellite Communications Station* with its huge saucer-shaped receivers picks up signals beamed earthwards by satellites. It is used for telecommunications and for the transmission of television pictures from all over the world.

St Kew   2B

Village off A39, 4m NE of Wadebridge, 9m SW of Camelford

Old slate cottages, a friendly inn, a Georgian vicarage and a parish church by a stream: all the ingredients of a perfect Cornish village. The 15th-c. **Church of St Kewa** retains its original roofs and some of the bench ends. The royal arms of Charles II and the letter of thanks to a loyal village are similar to those seen in many other churches in the area: so too the carved slate memorials to local squires. Among Cornwall's parish churches, the medieval stained glass here is second only to that of St Neot. Most vivid are the scenes of the Passion (E window, N aisle) and the Tree of Jesse (E window, S aisle).

St Keyne   3C

Village on B3254, 3m S of Liskeard

The lovely Old Mill houses the **Paul Corin Musical Collection** of old 'automatic instruments' such as barrel organs, pianolas and cafe orchestrions. The fairground organs are the most colourful, but all are in working order and perform surprisingly varied music.

St Keyne Holy Well, 1m S down the Causeland Road, was once famous because its waters were said to ensure that of a married couple, whichever partner drank first would be the dominant. In the 19th c. bottled water from the well used to sell rapidly at fairs and weddings! Today it is brackish and only the most superstitious would even taste it.

St Mawes   4B

Town on S coast (A3078), 3m E of Falmouth (by ferry). EC Wed

A sailing town, beautifully situated opposite Falmouth on the Carrick Roads at the mouth of Percuil Creek. It is dominated by the Renaissance **St Mawes Castle** built by King Henry VIII in 1540-43 to match Pendennis Castle on the other side of the estuary as a defence against the French. The castle is arranged in the form of a clover-leaf and is entered on the landward side by a drawbridge. Its excellent preservation

is due to the fact that (unlike the heroically defended Pendennis) it was surrendered by the Royalists in the Civil War without a shot being fired.

The town is built up in terraces from the harbour, and in the cottages near the water can be seen old St Mawes – a borough since 1562. The railway never reached the town and consequently it never enjoyed the prosperity of some of its neighbours in the 19th c. It has, accordingly, remained unspoilt.

St Mawgan   2B

Village off A3059/B3276, 6m NE of Newquay

Idyllically situated in the Vale of Lanherne, this is a perfect Cornish village, with a stream, old cottages and an inn. The 17th-c. granite manor house *Lanherne*, once home of the Arundell family, has been a Carmelite convent since 1794. The *Church of St Mawgan*, with its large 15th-c. tower, has some brasses to the Arundells. At the end of the vale 2m further on the stream runs into *Mawgan Porth*, a good bathing beach.

St Michael's Mount (NT)   4D

Island off S coast (A394), 4m E of Penzance; access by causeway at low tide and ferry at high tide (operates in summer only)

One of Britain's most exciting and romantic sites, the history of St Michael's Mount is as old as inhabited Cornwall itself. In Iron Age times (and possibly before) it was an important harbour for tin and gold traders on the route between Ireland and the Mediterranean. In the 5th c. Cadoc, a Celtic saint, made a pilgrimage to the island after hearing of a local fisherman's vision of the Archangel Michael hovering above it. From then on evidence suggests that there may have been a small religious community on the island. Edward the Confessor gave the island to the famed Priory of Mont St Michel on the Brittany coast in France, and the monks established a Church and monastery here (1044), which bears a striking similarity to its French counterpart.

This important religious centre attracted pilgrims from all over the country. They were undeterred by the fortification of the island during the wars with the French, and the fact that it became a much fought-over place. Its role as a fortress superseded its religious importance, however, and in 1425 it was annexed by the Crown and the monks removed. During the Wars of the Roses the Earl of Oxford held the island for the Lancastrians (1473). 25 years later the pretender Perkin Warbeck used it as a base – leaving his wife here for safety – when he marched towards London claiming the throne from Henry VII. His wife was safe, but Warbeck was captured and later executed.

The Mount was an important look-out, and a signalling beacon on top of the church warned of the approaching Spanish Armada in 1588. In 1659 Colonel John St Aubyn, who had been maintaining a garrison on the Mount, purchased it. His descendants have lived on the island ever since, but gave it to the National Trust in 1954.

The Mount is reached by causeway at low tide and ferry at high tide. Facing the mainland is a sheltered harbour, deep enough for 500-ton ships at spring high tides but dry at low tide. By the harbour are a handful of cottages, but dominating the 200ft Mount is the St Aubyn home, built from the priory and castle buildings which date back to the 12th c. and integrated into a single private house in the 19th c. by J.P. St Aubyn – the architect responsible for restoring so many Cornish churches. There is an armoury, the *Chevy Chase Room*, so named for its 18th-c. hunting frieze in the old Monks' Refectory, and a terrace mounted with batteries of guns. The priory Lady Chapel was remodelled into the beautiful *Blue Drawing Rooms* in the 18th c. They are filled with exquisite Chippendale furniture. The *Church* at the heart of the castle dates from 1275 (the earlier one was destroyed by an earthquake) but was heavily restored in the last century. On top of its tower is a lantern which served as an important landmark for ships. See also **Marazion*.

St Neot
Village off A38, 6m NW of Liskeard
2C

A pretty village in a tree-shrouded valley bottom, on the river of the same name. The saint, who actually lived here in the 9th c., is also commemorated by the 15th-c. **St Neot's Church**.

The church has the most splendid stained glass of any parish church in the county. Some of it is 1830 restoration, but much (recoloured) survives of the early 16th c. Three windows of special quality are in the N aisle. These are the St George window (W end), the St Neot window (1st on N wall) depicting the life of the saint, and the Creation window (E end). Also in the church is a copy on board of a letter of thanks from Charles I, commending the villagers for their loyalty (N wall) and a finely carved slate tomb of the early 17th c. (N aisle). Outside the church is an ancient *cross*, probably 10th-c., with Celtic carving, and 1/4m upstream from the church is a *holy well* under a Victorian canopy.

1/2m S of the village are the *Carnglaze Slate Caverns*, slate quarries open to visitors. Two medieval *bridges* at the E and W ends of the parish are worthy of note. 1 1/2m W on the River Bedalder is *Panters Bridge* (early 15th-c.), by-passed by the modern road but used as a lay-by and picnic spot. 1m E at Treverbyn is another of the same date on the River Fowey, also by-passed.

E of St Neot the road follows the River Fowey past the beautiful *Golitha Falls* at Redgate, and then joins the Bolventor road across the moor. This road passes the *Siblyback Reservoir*, a popular place for boating and angling.

St Stephen
Village on A3058, 7m W of St Austell
3B

A mining village towards the W end of the china-clay country. The parish *Church* is a good all-granite building of 1425 with a large N aisle and Norman font.

1/2m W, along the A3058, is *Automobilia*, Cornwall's motor museum. On display are 50 vintage cars, some dating back to the turn of the century, and almost all in working order.

St Tudy 2C
Village on Bodmin Moor off B3266, 8m N of Bodmin

A pleasant village in the midst of a network of country lanes, worth a diversion for its craft shops. The 15th-c. **Church of St Tudy**, restored in 1873, has a Norman font and some fine carved slate memorial tablets (16th-17th-c.). There are many splendid old granite and slate manor houses in the parish: one, *Tremeer*, has a 6-acre garden open by appointment. 1m NE of the village off the B3266 on the way to Michaelstow is *Bear Oak Gardens*, a small working farm open to the public with a mill pond and leat, animals, and a collection of herbs and plants useful to man.

Saltash 3D
Town on A38, 2m NW of Plymouth. Events: Fair Weekend (May), Regatta (Jun)

Although partly spoilt by overflow housing and suburbs from Plymouth, Saltash is not without Cornish charm. Of greatest interest are the two bridges. The *Prince Albert Railway Bridge*, built as it proudly says at each end by 'I. K. Brunel, Engineer, 1859', is a pioneering combination of suspension and arched support on granite pillars. Beside it is the more elegant *Suspension Bridge* (1961) for road traffic.

Before the road bridge was built, a ferry had crossed the River Tamar for 700 years, and beside the old jetty is the ancient *Old Boatman Inn*, now deprived of all its passing trade and all the pleasanter for that. In Fore Street Hill, leading down to the jetty, are a few old houses and the small but charming *Town Hall* of 1870.

Sancreed 4C
Village off A30, 4m W of Penzance

The parish of Sancreed offers a lot to the visitor although the village itself is only small. The road to the village from the A30 passes the *Drift Reservoir*, the most westerly reservoir in the country, providing water for Penzance. There is a pleasant picnic site, complete with tables and chairs, overlooking it. Fishing permits are available.

St Credan's Church is dedicated to the Cornish saint who abandoned a worldly life after killing his father and became a swineherd, a task he undertook with such piety that he was sanctified. The church is a 15th-c. granite building, but there are five Celtic crosses in the churchyard, all between 800-1200 years old, suggesting that this is a very ancient religious site.

2m W of the village, reached only by an exceedingly tortuous lane is **Carn Euny, an ancient British village**. Like nearby *Chysauster* this is a settlement of courtyard houses built of stone in the 1st c. BC. Archeological evidence shows that the site had been occupied by farmers living in wooden huts since at least the 6th c. BC. Four houses are uncovered, but the most interesting structure is the 66ft long *fogou* or underground chamber-tunnel. It has a paved floor and a circular domed chamber reached through a short passage. The function of the *fogou* is unknown: for storage, for defensive purposes or for religious ritual?

Between the village and Carn Euny, reached only by footpath, is *Caer Bran*, a hill with an Iron Age fort topping it, from which there are excellent views on clear days.

Sennen 4C
Village on A30, 1m E of Land's End

A remarkably unspoilt village, considering its proximity to the great tourist attraction of *Land's End*. Apart from the odd caravan site, there is little more than two admirable pubs and a church. **St Senan's** is the westernmost church in the country. The next parish west is in the United States. The church (13th-c. with 15th-c. tower and S aisle) is unusual for having only one transept – the N one, which now houses the organ. Of the two inns, *The First And Last* is the more famous, and – in view of that reputation – pleasantly uncommercialised. *The Wrecker's Inn* is named after the wreckers who used to live by looting shipwrecks on this lethal coast. There are stories of treacherous men who put false lights on cliff-tops to lure ships onto the rocks and of the parson who prayed not that ships should be wrecked, but that if they were, that it should happen in his parish. When he came to Land's End, George Fox, the founder of Quakerism, was horrified to find that people were so concerned to strip wrecks of their valuables that they would callously let the survivors drown.

½m NW on the shore is **Sennen Cove**, an attractive row of stone cottages tucked beneath the bracken-covered cliffs, and a little jetty. The lifeboat station is a reminder that while a few Cornishmen may have been wreckers, others have risked their lives to save seamen. There is a long silver-sand beach with rolling breakers ideal for surfing.

Stratton   1C
Town on A39, ½m E of Bude

On a hill overlooking Bude, the old town of Stratton has attractive steep streets with slate-roofed and thatched cottages and a Georgian market hall. On the top of the hill is the 15th-c. **St Andrew's Church**, with an E window designed by Burne-Jones. In the porch is an old prison door patterned in nails with the word 'CLINK'. Inside, the church retains its wooden barrel roofs with carved bosses. Note also the royal arms of Charles II in the N aisle chapel, testifying to the loyalty of the parish to the monarchy in the Civil War. Another reminder of Stratton's Royalist sympathies is in the old *Tree Inn* down the hill, a charming pub with Tudor fireplace and timbering. This was once the manor house of the Grenvilles, who fought the Parliamentarians at Stamford Hill. Near the town is the site of the famous battle (1643), a victory for the Royalists.

Tintagel   2C
Village on B3263, 20m W of Launceston

This village on the rugged N coast has grown out of all resemblance to the remote parish of a few decades ago: the result of the promotion of the Arthurian legend centred on the nearby Tintagel Castle. Geoffrey of Monmouth started it

Tintagel Castle

all in the 12th c. with the idea that the Celtic King Arthur, hero of the wars against the Saxons, was born in a fortress on the site of the present castle in the 6th c. The legend, enlarged by the poems of Tennyson and the paintings of Turner, ensured constant pilgrimage to the site after the railway came to Camelford in the 1890s.

Of the old village, little now remains except the remarkable **Old Post Office** (adm fee). Built in the 14th c., this is a fascinating survival of medieval domestic architecture, with its 3ft-thick slate walls, granite doorway and heavily tiled, sway-backed roof. Other buildings of less antiquity promote the Arthurian legend: notably *King Arthur's Hall* with its reconstruction of banqueting hall, Round Table, etc. Outside the village the old parish **Church of St Merteriana**, set in isolation on the windswept Glebe Cliff, is worth a diversion. The Saxon and early-Norman church, restored in the 1880s, is cruciform, with an aisleless nave and long transepts. It has an unusual five-legged Norman font and a 15th-c. rood screen.

Tintagel Castle is reached by footpath from the village. It is located partly on the mainland and partly on a narrow-necked headland, almost an island, between two cliffs preserved by the National Trust. The best approach is to leave the main path at the second bridge over the stream and follow the track along the side of the ravine to the mainland section of the castle. Here is the gate into the *Lower Ward* (the *Upper Ward*, above, with its impressive *Round Hall*, has been partially lost in rock falls).

The castle was built in the 12th-13th c. with 15th-c. additions, so is not contemporary with Arthur. There was, however, a 6th-c. Celtic monastery on the site, part of which can still be seen on the headland. To reach the headland, a flight of steps is descended, with views down to *Merlin's Cave* and a bathing beach, and a second flight ascended to the *Inner Ward*. (The two parts of the castle were once connected

by a bridge.) The gateway at the top, a 19th-c. reconstruction, leads into the *Great Hall*, with surviving 12th-c. walls. On the summit of the headland the Norman *Chapel* can be seen; on the slopes below the outlines of the buildings of the 6th-c. *Monastery*.

2m S of Tintagel is *Trebarwith Strand*, exposed at low tide, which offers good bathing and surfing. In the 19th c. vessels were beached here to load slate from the local quarries based on Treknow. The river valley which runs down here is particularly dramatic, with its eroded volcanic rock. N of Tintagel is a walk to the headlands of Willapark and Lye Rock (see **Bossiney*).

Tregony 3B
Village on A3078, 10m E of Truro

Until the River Fal silted up completely, Tregony was an important port and for a while one of the most powerful boroughs in Cornwall. It predates Truro and Falmouth. Now it is a quiet village with a single wide street climbing steeply from the river. At the bottom are some delightful *almshouses* of 1696 (rebuilt 1895) on granite pillars 'for poor housekeepers'. Higher up is the old *Town Hall* (now an antique shop) and the detached *clock tower* of 1846 – all evidence of the town's former glory.

Trelissick Gardens (NT) 3B
Gardens off B3289, 4m S of Truro

The beautiful gardens and deciduous woods run down to the River Fal. From the gardens – planted with rare shrubs – and woodland paths are tantalising views of the water, where large cargo ships can generally be seen laid up. The Greek-style mansion is not open to the public.

Trelowarren 4A
Historic house off B3293, 6m SE of Helston

Owned by the Vyvyan family since 1427, Trelowarren is a large rambling house whose oldest parts date back to 1450 but which has been continually added to in the succeeding five centuries. Part of the building has been converted into flats, but some of the more interesting rooms as well as the chapel are open to the public. There is a lively programme each year of exhibitions, concerts and lectures, all of which are advertised locally.

Trengwainton Gardens (NT) 4C
Gardens off A3071, 2m NW of Penzance

The extensive shrub gardens around *Trengwainton House* (which is of no special interest and not open to the public) were laid out in the first half of the 19th c. and remodelled in 1925. The mild climate encourages rare Asian and Australian plants not found in gardens elsewhere in Britain. There are fine views of Mount Bay.

Trerice see *Newquay*

Trewint Cottage 2C
Historic house on A30, 10m SW of Launceston

A delightful little 18th-c. cottage, just sufficient distance from the A30 to be very peaceful. Here Digory and Elizabeth Isbell lived and were hosts to John Wesley, the founder of Methodism. They were so impressed by his preaching that they built on two rooms to their cottage expressly for him to use on his frequent visits to Cornwall (1743-89). Today the first floor room serves as the smallest Methodist hall in the country, and downstairs there is a small collection of Wesley memorabilia. There is an intimate memorial garden. The Isbells are buried in the beautiful churchyard at *Altarnun*, ¼m N.

Trewithen see *Probus*

Truro 3A/3B
Pop 15,690 9m E of Redruth (A390) EC Thur MD Wed Inf: Tel (0872) 74555

Cornwall's only city, Truro is also the seat of the County Council and recognised as the administrative centre of the county.

William the Conqueror established a castle here after suppressing the Saxon uprisings, but by the time of Henry II it was ruined. Its closeness to the coast meant that Truro, like so many

places in Cornwall, had the misfortune of being raided and looted by the French in the Middle Ages. Despite the attacks and lack of defences, Truro was an important tin-exporting and Stannary town, only declining in the 19th c. when the superior port at Falmouth stole much of its trade. Although the 18th c. was not a prosperous time for the town, there was a great deal of building and its best streets – which give it the attractive air of Dublin or Bristol – date from the latter part of the century. Truro was made a city in 1877 and three years later the Prince of Wales (later King Edward VII) laid the foundation stone of the cathedral. Today Truro is a busy and prosperous city, the focus for the surrounding countryside and especially lively on market day (Wednesday).

The **Cathedral**, the first Protestant cathedral to be built since St Paul's, was designed by J.L. Pearson and erected between 1880-1910 in the Early English style. As in a French town, the cathedral is placed in the crowded streets without a close or green, which makes it unlike any other English cathedral. The *West Towers* (the SW tower is named after Edward VII and the NW after Princess Alexandra) are 204ft high and the Normandy Gothic-style tower and spire over the crossing, known as the *Victoria Tower*, is 250ft high.

Standing at the W end, the interior seems cool, airy and austere. This effect was brilliantly achieved by Pearson in a number of subtle ways. First the nave is built of cream-coloured Somerset stone, but the choir is local blue-grey granite. Secondly there is no screen separating the choir from the nave, so there is an uninterrupted view to the altar: this is most unusual. Thirdly the Early English style of very tall unbroken columns and stone-ribbed vaulting contributes a feeling of space. And fourthly, Pearson was sparing in the use of colour and decoration. Everywhere is bare stone and unpainted wood.

Visitors should look for the painted alabaster memorial to John Robartes (d.

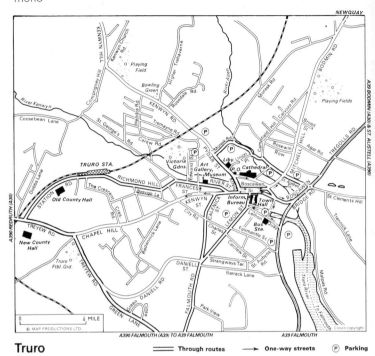

NEWQUAY

A39 BODMIN (A30) & ST AUSTELL (A390)

A390 REDRUTH (A30)

A390 FALMOUTH (A39) TO A39 FALMOUTH · A39 FALMOUTH

© MAP PRODUCTIONS LTD.

Crown copyright

Truro

━━━ Through routes   ⟶ One-way streets   ⓟ Parking

1614) and his wife in the *N transept*. Robartes, a mayor of Truro, founded the fortunes of the family of merchants who built *★Lanhydrock*. Note also the fine rose windows over the galleries of this and the *S transept*. At the entrance to the *N choir aisle* is a fine *terracotta panel* of The Road to Calvary by George Tinworth, with beautifully modelled figures.

The *choir* floor is Italian marble in a fine mosaic design, and the stalls are Burmese teak. The magnificent carved *reredos* is made of Bath stone. The elaborate *bishop's chair* is flanked by chaplains' chairs.

The *S choir aisle* is all that remains of the 15th-c. St Mary's Parish Church, demolished when the cathedral was built. It is cleverly linked, and the iron railings are particularly handsome. The organ is one of Father Willis' last and is famous for its superb tone. The stained

glass windows, by Bell and Clayton, represent the 'Hand of God' sequence.

Returning to the W end of the cathedral by the *S aisle*, the *baptistry* is a striking feature with its fine Gothic vaulting and ornate font cover. Further down the aisle is a commemorative window to John Wesley.

On the N side of the cathedral is a small garden, on land intended for cloisters which were never built as a result of the First World War. In their place is a flat-roofed rectangular *chapter house* of 1966.

The other main historical attraction of Truro lies in its Georgian streets. There are numerous fine individual Georgian houses but the best ensemble is *Lemon Street* (1800), a beautiful hill street of three-storey pastel-coloured houses. It is particularly fine viewed from the top, with the cathedral in the background. To the W of Lemon Street, the short curved *Walsingham Place* is also good. The rest of Truro is very pleasant, with few ugly modern blocks and many terraces of simple two-storey working-men's 19th-c. cottages.

The **County Museum and Art Gallery** (River Street) is famous for its collection of Cornish minerals. Also the De Pass collection of old master drawings. The *Truro Pottery* in Chapel Hill, in existence for over 200 years, is famous for its earthenware and has a small exhibition area as well as a shop. Truro is an excellent shopping centre with all the major stores and a regular market.

4m S are the beautiful **Trelissick Gardens* (NT), and beyond them, across the King Harry Ferry, the churchyard of **St Just-in-Roseland*, the most beautiful in England. In summer there are cruises down the Fal to **Falmouth*.

2m SE is *Malpas*, an attractive spot at the confluence of the Truro and Tresillian rivers. *The Heron* inn overlooks an idyllic riverside scene, with thickly-wooded banks and a heronry.

Wadebridge 2B
Town on A39, 8m SE of Padstow, 7m NW of Bodmin. Event: Royal Cornwall Show (Jun)

At the head of the Camel estuary, this town boasts the longest **bridge** in Cornwall, the only way through for traffic on the N coast travelling to Padstow or Newquay. 320ft long, the bridge has 17 arches and was built in the 15th c. It has since been twice enlarged, in 1847 and 1962-3. Its popular name, 'The Bridge on Wool' is attributed to the legend that it was built on bales of wool. The bridge was originally 510ft long, which shows how the Camel has silted up over the years. The old wharves and quays are further evidence that this was once a busy port: similarly the old railway buildings record the days when coal, timber, sand and agricultural produce were important cargoes.

There is a beautiful walk from Wadebridge to **Padstow* along the Camel Estuary, following the course of the old railway line (5m, return by bus).

Warbstow Bury 2C
Ancient site off A395, 15m NW of Launceston

½m W of the village of Warbstow is this impressive earthwork, with a double rampart, commanding splendid views of Bodmin and Dartmoor. In the middle of a long barrow is a 'giant's grave', believed by some to be the burial place of King Arthur.

Warleggan 2C
Village on Bodmin Moor between A30 and A38, 12m NW of Liskeard. Event: Carnival (Jun)

Reached via Mount, on the Cardinham-St Neot road, this has been described as the loneliest village on Bodmin Moor (the Cornish name means 'high place'). Although it now shares a rector with Cardinham, there has been a church here for 800 years. St Bartholomew's is of special interest as half of it (the nave) is the original 12th-c. church, with a N wall built of rubble (note also the Norman window near the tower). The other half of the church, the S aisle, is built of granite, which came into use for building in the 15th c. The low granite tower, also 15th-c., once supported a steeple, which fell down when struck by lightning in 1818.

The isolation of the spot had its effect on the last incumbent, the Rev. Densham (1931-53), who developed an acute distrust of the outside world. He refused to hold normal services, and put barbed wire round the rectory grounds. To compensate for no congregation he put cardboard effigies in the pews.

Wendron 4A
Village on B3297, 3m NE of Helston

The **Poldark Mine**, known as the *Wheal Roots Mine* when tin was still being extracted, is now open to the public as a museum of mining. The tunnels, chambers, lodes and seams can be seen and there are also displays of mining machinery and domestic equipment.

Wheal Martyn Museum 3B
Open air museum on A391, 2m N of St Austell

In the heart of the lunar landscape of china-clay pits and spoil heaps this fascinating museum shows the history of the china-clay industry. There is an excellent audio-visual presentation and waterwheels (one 35ft diameter), 'mica-drags', wagons, pumps and two static steam locomotives which demonstrate the brilliant feats employed by Victorian and earlier engineers to extract the china-clay or kaolin. There is a café and shop selling pottery (including porcelain and bone china made from kaolin).

Zennor 4C

Village on B3306, 5m W of St Ives

Despite its exposed position on Penwith's Atlantic coast, Zennor has been a place of settlement from Neolithic times. The present granite village, lying just off the main road, was built by the tin miners. **St Senara's Church**, with its solid tower at the W end, dominates the village. Originally 12th-c., the church is a 19th-c. restoration, with scraped interior walls and modern fittings. The N aisle, constructed at the time, took out the N transept of the original church. A surviving detail is an old bench end, probably 15th-c., carved with the figure of a mermaid.

Adjoining the old mill-house by the bridge is the *Folk Museum*, with a re-creation of a Cornish kitchen, mining, farming and milling tools, and other interesting objects reflecting the harsh life of the locals. It was a life, however, which had its romantic appeal. One of the outsiders who saw the attractions of the place was D.H. Lawrence, who wrote *Women in Love* while living at Higher Tregarthen. Unfortunately it was during the First World War, and Lawrence's German wife Frieda was suspected of being a spy. Local hostility – and a police order – eventually forced them to leave.

The most famous monument to prehistoric settlement hereabouts is the **Zennor Quoit**, reached by a track off the main road 1m E of the village. Here the huge capstone, 18 x 9½ft, has fallen from its five supporting uprights. (The additional upright stones belonged to an antechamber.) The stone barrow which originally covered the structure was 40ft across.

1m from the village is *Zennor Head*, one of the most spectacular headlands on this forbidding coast. When the sea is rough the spray can shoot 100ft into the air from a 'blow hole'. Another dramatic headland to the W is *Gurnard's Head*, with remains of an Iron Age cliff fort with three ramparts and ruins of a medieval chapel.

Zennor

Index